Books by Robert Traver

Fiction

ANATOMY OF A MURDER
DANNY AND THE BOYS
HORNSTEIN'S BOY
LAUGHING WHITEFISH

Nonfiction

TROUBLESHOOTER
SMALL TOWN D.A.
TROUT MADNESS
ANATOMY OF A FISHERMAN

THE
JEALOUS
MISTRESS

THE
JEALOUS
MISTRESS

ROBERT TRAVER

LITTLE, BROWN AND COMPANY · BOSTON · TORONTO

LIBRARY OF CONGRESS CATALOG CARD NO. 67–28226

SECOND PRINTING

Published simultaneously in Canada
by Little, Brown & Company (Canada) Limited

PRINTED IN THE UNITED STATES OF AMERICA

To Henry M. Bates

The law is a jealous mistress.

— Author probably unknown, the phrase being variously attributed to numerous old-time lawyers, judges and legal scholars, including the Englishman Roger North in 1824 and the American Joseph Story in 1829.

Preface

SINCE of litigation, like war, there is no end, and since judges have rarely been notable for reticence or brevity of utterance, and since a vast quantity of their rhetoric becomes embalmed in books — the bound and numbered reports of legal cases that are the backbone of any journeyman lawyer's library — and since this torrent has continued unabated for centuries, including some of the oldest surviving books in English, pretty soon there isn't going to be any place left for the poor lawyer to sit. . . .

In their staggering totality these law reports are a monument to man's will to survive and prevail, to his infinite capacity for folly and conflict, for greed and perversity, for mischief and rue, and also to his fleeting moments of compassion and grandeur.

This vast accumulation is an almost untapped reservoir of some of the most absorbing stories on earth. For in sober truth every legal case that ever happened is essentially a story, the story of aroused, pulsing, actual people fighting each other or the state for *something:* for money, for property, for power, pride, honor, love, freedom, even for life — and quite often, one suspects, for the pure unholy joy of fighting. Yet most of these lawbooks are rarely dusted off and read, and then only by lawyers and judges and occasional delving law professors and students. For the rest of us they might just as well have been inscribed in Sanskrit, sealed in a space capsule, and shot to the moon; we are scarcely aware of their existence, let alone of what's in them. In this book I propose to raid this great neglected boneyard of human striving and conflict and to disinter a few of the legal cases, ancient and modern, that have especially interested me and which I hope may interest, entertain, and even mildly enlighten the general reader. In fact they make my book.

If this book must have a message I warily suggest that it might run something like this: that it shows the remarkable continuity of the law, whose stored wisdom from the experience of centuries can be tapped in a trice; that it shows the equally remarkable resilience of the law in adapting and extending old rules and concepts to unforeseen new situations and to changing and even explosive times and mores; that it possibly shows, contrary to the popular notion, that our judges and lawyers are in the vanguard of those unsung foot soldiers who guard and protect our hard-won liberties; that, most simply stated, it shows that the law is the difference between a debate and an alley fight; and, finally, that it shows that however chaotic and uncertain modern life may appear, we still live by the rule of law. This last, upon reflection, may be one of our greatest claims to being moderately civilized.

I should add that in quoting from or referring to actual judicial opinions, as I do throughout, I have frequently used ellipses, brackets, paraphrase, and other sly means to avoid repetition and legal technicality, to achieve brevity, and to omit matter possibly relevant to the opinion but not to my inquiry. Sometimes I did this for sneakier reasons. While it is undeniable that in judicial writing it is frequently hard to be succinct, it is equally undeniable that the sedative effect of some judicial opinions is awesome, sometimes — let's face it — approaching outright coma. So I must confess that I have occasionally used some of these writing stratagems simply (and hopefully) to get the message across without also inducing sleep.

ROBERT TRAVER

Acknowledgments

ACKNOWLEDGMENT and thanks are due the following: the law library of the University of Michigan, the law library of the Marquette County (Michigan) Bar Association, and the libraries of the following law firms: Mayer, Friedlich, Spiess, Tierney, Brown & Platt of Chicago and Clancey & Hansen of my home town, in the last of which I did most of my research and in all of which I did some. I also thank those lawyers and other men of the law who variously helped me, only a few of whom are named in the text. I thank Louis Lusky, one of the principal lawyers in Sam Thompson's case and now a professor of law at Columbia University, for patiently checking and correcting my statement of facts in that case. I also thank Alfred J. Lewis of the Law School and law library of the University of Michigan for his many gracious benefactions, among them, verifying my citations and tracking down the probable source of the title and epigraph. I also wish to thank the *Michigan State Bar Journal* for permission to reprint several of these chapters which first appeared in that publication. Lastly, I should like to thank the authors, editors and publishers of all of the lawbooks and reports I consulted, ancient and modern, and particularly the editors and publishers of the *American Law Reports* series (The Lawyers Co-Operative Publishing Company and Bancroft-Whitney Company) for the invaluable suggestions and assistance their many superb legal annotations gave me.

Contents

Contents

THE
JEALOUS
MISTRESS

I

Uncle Tom's Granddaughter

G NAWED with envy am I by those iron-willed fellow lawyers who can bore into the research of a legal problem with all the deadly concentration of a beagle hot on the trail of a rabbit; alas, I cannot. When I look up law I am more like those addled souls who, when they consult a dictionary, usually wind up with every definition but the one they seek. In fact this weakness of mine probably accounts for the writing of this book; it's pretty much how I stumbled across most of these cases, including the one that follows.

One day some years ago, when I was a black-robed judge, I had occasion to consult one of the amendments to the Federal Constitution. I can't now remember which one it was, except that it certainly wasn't the venerable one against slavery, which naturally I shortly found myself absorbedly reading, annotations and all. "Neither slavery nor involuntary servitude," I read, "shall exist within the United States or any place subject to their jurisdiction."

"How quaint," I mused. "How quaint that our constitution should remain cluttered with such obsolete stuff. Why don't they weed it out?" I glanced idly at the cases collected in the footnotes. There weren't many and — let's see — most of them seemed to involve people in Southern or border states

shortly after the Civil War. And what was it I was supposed
to be looking up? But the will-o'-the-wisp had got me and I
read on. Suddenly my eyes were glued to the page. Or then
again perhaps they were riveted. "California, 1947," I read in
the fine print. "Motion for new trial of defendant convicted of
slavery denied. See *United States v. Rowe,* 73 Fed. Supp. 76."
I looked again. There must be some mistake. Slavery in
1947! I must do the thoughtful thing and write the editor
about this droll typo. Surely a case of *slavery* could not possibly have existed in our emancipated twentieth century. But
there it was. "California, 1947," I read again. Maybe I had
better first read the case itself before I chided the editor.
After all, anything might and frequently did happen in that
curious commonwealth. I shook my head and got up and
went over to the sagging shelves of my systematically unread
lawbooks. I found and pulled down Volume 73 of the *Federal
Supplement* and blew the dust off and sank into a chair and
turned to page 76 and began reading. When I was done I
thoughtfully closed the book and laid it on my lap and uttered
a low whistle, the kind of whistle favored, I believe, by the
soapier soap operas. It was all too true; there was no mistake;
almost a hundred years after it had legally been banished, an
actual case of slavery had existed in our vaunted twentieth
century.

The story that the case unfolded was bizarre to the point of
unbelief. In 1946 an elderly woman called Mary Rowe was
charged with holding a Negro woman called Dora Jones as a
slave, contrary to the Constitution and supporting federal
statutes. At the trial, which was held in federal court in California, the prosecution showed that the defendant had kept
Dora Jones in her household as a maidservant for many
years; that during all this time Dora was required to arise at
an early hour and perform all of the laborious and menial
household chores. She was forbidden to leave the house except on express errands. She had no days off and no vacation.
She invariably slept in the poorest quarters and her food con-

sisted mainly of table scraps and leavings. It was shown that on occasion she was beaten; that she was denied any opportunity to make friends; and that once when a relative visited her she was required to send the relative away. During all this time she received no compensation whatever.

The government monotonously recounted its astounding revelations. Once when Dora had protested her lot and had spoken of leaving, the defendant Mary Rowe had angrily reminded her of an adulterous relationship that had existed nearly forty years before between the maidservant Dora — then a young girl in her teens — and the defendant's late husband, long since dead. Mary Rowe also reminded Dora of the abortion that had followed this ancient backstairs romance. She threatened to have Dora committed to prison or an insane asylum if she tried to leave. After that, whenever Dora grew restive. Mary Rowe conjured up the goblins of the past and repeated her threats. Frightened, Dora stayed on.

In the fall of 1946 there was one interlude of freedom for Dora. It was very brief. Mary Rowe decided to take a cross-country automobile trip. Included in her party were her own grown daughter and, of course, the hapless maidservant Dora Jones. During the long trip Dora was required to sleep at night in the car. Mary Rowe's daughter finally rebelled at this cruel treatment and early one morning persuaded Dora to set out with her to find the police. Mary Rowe caught up with them and repeated her old threats and induced fearful Dora to return to her bondage. That night, for her punishment, Dora was required to sleep on the floor of the hotel room occupied by her mistress.

Later Mary Rowe pushed on to a luxurious California resort. During all of her stay there — nearly a month — Dora was not only required to serve her mistress hand and foot but was also obliged to sleep at night in the car parked on a public street. (Mary Rowe, you see, was no spendthrift.) Finally, Mary Rowe took a house near this resort and Dora continued to work for her without compensation.

One fateful night Dora was allowed to baby-sit for some neighbors. When she got home Mary Rowe accosted her and took the money away from her. This was the straw that broke the camel's back; once again Dora fled to the police — and this time she made it. After hearing her strange story the police went into action. The federal authorities were called in; Mary Rowe was arrested and prosecuted for slavery and finally convicted by a jury and duly punished for her sins.

The lawbook fell from my lap. I walked over to the window and took off my glasses and stared sightlessly down at the toiling traffic. What had our old law school dean told us legal fledglings in his farewell graduation talk so many years ago? Ah, it was coming back. "I shall conclude my remarks with a platitude," he had said. "Young men, remember that eternal vigilance is the price of freedom." He had paused and his gray eyes had flashed and there was an edge of steel in his voice. "And always remember this, too — of selfish scoundrels in this old world there will never be any shortage. Smite them wherever you find them. Good luck and good-bye."

One had been smitten in California.

2

Justice Unshackled

THE charge was rape, and Ernest Coursolle sat whisper-
ing to his lawyer at the defense table in the district court
for Yellow Medicine County, Minnesota. His trial was about
to begin. He had been charged with taking part in what was
claimed to be the gang rape of an eighteen-year-old girl. Two of
his alleged companions in the affair, McLafferty and Collins,
were already serving penal terms for rape of the same girl
during the same general period, and Coursolle's lawyer had
served the necessary papers to have them brought from confinement to court to testify for his client.

The jury was already chosen and in its place, ready and
waiting. One bored juror was surreptitiously reading a folded
newspaper that lay on his lap. The prosecutor sat at his table,
occasionally yawning and shuffling papers and impatiently
consulting his wristwatch. A bailiff glided in with a pitcher of
water for the judge, who poured a glassful and sipped it and
pushed the glass away, making a wry face. The bailiff, a sensitive soul, hurried out a side door and returned with a pitcher
of ice cubes. His Honor tried again and sat back, smiling at
no one in particular.

A heavy rear door breathed open and two men dressed like
workmen were ushered in by the sheriff. Both men were

handcuffed and their handcuffs were in turn chained to their
belts so they could not raise their arms. The sheriff led the
two men to a row of chairs inside the railing dividing the back
benches from the working area of the court, where they sat
with bowed heads, the jury meanwhile studying them curiously. These men were McLafferty and Collins, summoned
from confinement as witnesses by the defendant Coursolle.

The judge tapped his gavel lightly and leaned forward and
addressed the prosecutor. "Is the State ready to proceed?" he
inquired.

The prosecutor popped to his feet and said, "Yes, Your
Honor."

"Is the defense ready?" the judge next inquired.

The defendant's lawyer arose and stood brooding a moment and then ventured to tell the judge he thought that the
two waiting witnesses ought to be unshackled; that while he
was unprepared to argue this unexpected contingency, he
rather thought the law was that not only the defendant but his
witnesses had the right to appear in court unshackled; that
otherwise the jury might become prejudiced against their testimony, and his client might thereby be denied his constitutional right to a fair trial.

His Honor pondered this for a moment and spoke. "Are
you otherwise prepared to go ahead?"

"Yes, Your Honor," the defense lawyer said.

"Then the trial will proceed," His Honor ordered, and so it
did, the shackles and handcuffs still restraining the two waiting witnesses. The trial dragged along, as trials do, but I shall
not report it in detail for two reasons: it forms no proper part
of what I am trying to tell in this essay and anyway the reported case does not go into detail and I don't want to go
behind it. In a general way one gathers that part of the defense was that the defendant did not rape the girl and that any
intercourse that may have occurred was with the consent of
the victim, who allegedly relished the encounter.

Meanwhile the defendant's lawyer had evidently been hitting the books; on the third day of the trial at the opening of the morning session, he arose and cleared his throat and addressed the judge. "Your Honor," he said, "at this time I want the record to show that the two witnesses . . . are manacled in court, and that this is in violation of State law . . . and I demand that the sheriff immediately remove those manacles and that the jury be instructed not to be prejudiced by the fact that the sheriff of this county has violated the State law."

"Show me your authority," the judge ordered.

The defendant's lawyer thereupon showed the judge a state statute bearing on the subject, but His Honor was unimpressed and ordered the trial to proceed. The manacles remained, the defendant's lawyer noting an exception on the record that repeated much of what he had just said.

On the morning of the fourth day the defendant's lawyer arose and made still another statement: "May the record show," he said, "that during the entire day yesterday the two witnesses . . . were . . . in the presence of the jury manacled with a short chain attached to the handcuffs, and this . . . chain attached to a belt around their bodies just over the hips, so that their hands were close to their private parts, and they were unable to wipe their faces . . . and they are now being exhibited . . . before the jury in the same way."

At this juncture the prosecutor arose and pointed out to the judge that these men were prisoners serving time in penal institutions; that they had been brought to court under habeas corpus as witnesses for the defendant; and that the sheriff was keeping them handcuffed under advice from the officials of the penal institutions from whence they came. To this statement the defense attorney promptly objected on the ground that there was no proper showing that these witnesses had to be kept under any such restraint. The speeches over, and the witnesses remaining manacled, the trial dragged on to its conclusion. The only time the two witnesses were unchained, one gathers, was when they respectively took the stand to testify for the defendant. They might have saved their breath — the defendant Coursolle was promptly convicted of rape by the jury and sentenced to prison.

On his appeal the defendant urged many grounds for reversal, among the principal ones being the business of the state's keeping his two witnesses manacled. Mr. Justice Gallagher, after stating the background facts, beamed in tersely upon this contention:

"Under the early common law when a prisoner was brought into court for trial upon his plea of not guilty to an indictment for a criminal offense he was entitled to make his appearance free from all shackles or bonds. This is an existing right in the United States. . . . It is the spirit of the law that a prisoner upon his trial before a jury shall have the unrestrained use of his limbs and must not be compelled to suffer any physical bonds or burdens which might confuse or embarrass his mental faculties. A defendant has the right to have his witnesses unmanacled for the same reason that he is allowed to be unmanacled. The right also extends to the arraignment, the selection of a jury, and all other periods of the trial."

Warming to his task he continued: "It is our opinion under the record here that the court should have ordered the manacles removed from defendant's two witnesses. It seems obvious that the appearance of the manacled witnesses in court day after day would create an effect that would be prejudicial to defendant's right to a fair trial. The old adage that 'a man is known by the company he keeps' could easily produce an inflammatory situation so far as the jury was concerned as a result of the accused's principal witnesses being handcuffed each day during the trial. After all, the accused, whether guilty or innocent, was entitled to a fair trial and it is the duty of the trial court, the county attorney, and even the sheriff to see that he gets one by preventing any conduct or situations during the trial which prejudice the accused in the minds of the jury." His Honor then pointed out that while the trial court may keep a prisoner shackled "if it is manifest that such a precaution is necessary to prevent violence or escape," the court must have some reason, based upon the conduct of the prisoner at the time of the trial, to authorize the forfeiture of so important a right: "There must be some immediate necessity for the use of shackles. . . . We cannot find sufficient reason here. . . . Reversed and new trial granted."

The defendant got another crack at it.

ADDENDUM: I have since learned from William Sutor, one of the lawyers in the *Coursolle* case, that on the remand the rape charge was dismissed and a second-degree assault charge substituted to which the defendant pleaded guilty. He was sentenced to jail, but because of his confinement during the interim, he was summarily discharged from custody.

I learned about shackles the hard way. Back in the days when I was a dewy young district attorney, Michigan's "maximum security" prison was located, as it still is today, in my county. It consequently fell to my lot to prosecute all the criminal cases that emanated from this crowded institution. Since a good many emanated, it was a rare term of court that I didn't draw at least one little daisy I had to try, ranging anywhere from prison escape to first-degree murder.

Not only did I draw a number of cases from the prison but, it seems in retrospect, most of these prison defendants pleaded not guilty and demanded a full-dress trial regardless of the People's often overwhelming evidence of guilt. When a missing trusty gardener is found three days later, fly-bitten and hungry, hiding in a hayloft a hundred miles from his abandoned lawn mower, what *did* he have in mind if it wasn't escape? That's when I first learned about amnesia. Amnesia was always a great favorite with the escape boys — if rather less so with the juries who tried them.

I suspect the boys demanded their little trials mostly for a lark, for the sheer joy of the outing, the change of scenery, and also to keep their stable of "prison lawyers" alert —

some of whom seemed to know far more criminal law, I sometimes felt, than did the young district attorney himself. Aided by these prison Darrows, they would make all manner of erudite preliminary motions in their cases, many of which demanded separate pre-trial hearings, such as motions to quash the information or to suppress certain evidence. Thus in some cases a resourceful prisoner might wangle three or four trips to court before we got down to try the almost forgotten issue of guilt or innocence. I suppose, too, some of them kept in mind that there was always the chance, however slim, to make a break for it during these preliminary sashays up to circuit court.

That's how I met "Crazy Matt" Wyatt. One fine day I drew Crazy Matt, a prison inmate, on some sort of nonjury preliminary matter the precise nature of which I've long forgotten. But I'll never forget Crazy Matt. His hearing was set before Circuit Judge Glenn W. Jackson, now dead, a fine judge and lawyer, and my esteemed friend. Now Crazy Matt had previously escaped from virtually every prison in the state — and a few elsewhere — before in desperation he had been transferred to *my* prison, which so far had miraculously contrived to contain him. He had once even held the entire parole board as hostages during a wild attempted escape downstate. We *knew* all this, and when the prison guards delivered him into our hands, they solemnly urged the sheriff and me to be sure to keep him both manacled and leg-ironed during his brief nonjury hearing before Judge Jackson. "Bad, *bad* actor," they warned darkly. So crazy Matt was brought clanking into court and propped in place in the witness chair, fairly sagging under his burden of armor.

Judge Jackson observed all this and frowned and motioned the sheriff and me up to the other side of his bench.

"Why all the medieval hardware?" he whispered.

"Real dangerous customer, Judge," the sheriff whispered back. "The prison guards particularly warned us."

"But you men know I don't ever like that sort of thing in

my courtroom," the vexed judge whispered, pursing his lips
and shaking his head. He was a great stickler for judicial
precedent and courtroom decorum, bless him.

"But there's no jury here to see it," I pointed out, dimly
remembering some of my Freshman Crimes. "And certainly
you are entirely without prejudice, Your Honor," I suavely
added.

"I don't like it anyway. Remove the hardware," he ordered.

Allah had spoken, so we shrugged and the sheriff went out
and got a prison guard to come and unlock Crazy Matt — a
ritual almost as elaborate as opening a bank in the morning.
This done, Crazy Matt sat back, flexing his cramped wrists
and looking down at me at my table with the pent fury and
detached malevolence of a caged lion — or, worse yet, a lion
whose cage door had carelessly been left open. Then his darting eyes began casing all the exits in the courtroom.

The judge nodded at me to begin and I cleared my throat
to gain Crazy Matt's attention. Again his eyes locked with
mine, again flecked and aglint with a kind of cold impersonal
fury. "When will it happen?" I asked myself, sure that some
kind of eruption was imminent.

"Proceed," the judge prompted me.

"Yes, Your Honor."

I barely got to ask Crazy Matt his name when all hell broke
loose. He leaped from his chair and, declaiming wildly, like
an anarchist from his soap box, stunned us into inaction with
a swift hypnotic flow of rich old Anglo-Saxon invective. This
included some trenchant advice on what all of us might indi-
vidually forthwith proceed to do with ourselves. Then he
leaped nimbly over the front rail of the witness box and
dashed by me at full speed — I didn't move (after all, I reflected, my gifts were mostly those of the mind). Hurling a
farewell obscenity over his shoulder, he darted out the main
front door and clattered on down the wide marble stairs.

Meanwhile, the sheriff was tugging away at his hidden

shoulder holster like a man frantically scratching himself. Finally he produced a pistol which he pointed ominously aloft, as though he were about to assassinate one of the old crystal chandeliers. Then he remembered a shortcut through the clerk's office, and away he lumbered out a rear door, plaintively muttering to himself like a reproachful scoutmaster, "Hold on there, now. Just you hold on there."

His Honor sat looking down at me and I sat looking up at His Honor. Neither of us spoke. In the distance we could hear the sounds of running feet and muffled, barking shouts. Presently there was a quick series of pistol shots, loud and clear. I ran out the sheriff's door only to meet the sheriff and prison guards coming back with Crazy Matt, sheepish-looking and unharmed. The sheriff had shot at his legs — coming ever closer — and Matt had rapidly got the message and promptly deferred any escape plans until another day. I hurried back to report all this to His Honor.

I found the judge sitting very still up on the bench in the deserted courtroom. He seemed a little pale — as I was sure I was. I went around to the side and saw that he had lifted and was still holding his black silk gown off the floor — daintily, with two fingers of each hand — and that his feet were also at least two inches off the ground, like those of a maiden lady being terrorized by a mouse.

"Got him!" I announced, still panting and shaking.

"Dead?" he said.

"Nope, surrendered. Not a scratch." I affected a calm I did not feel. "Ah — shall we proceed with the hearing?"

Color and confidence were returning rapidly to the judge. He lowered his feet and his gown. "Of course, of course," he said gruffly. "Go tell 'em to fetch him in."

I paused at the courtroom door and turned back. "Hardware this time, Your Honor?" I inquired politely.

His Honor pondered a moment and then smiled at me ever so faintly. "Hardware this time," he ruled. *"All* of it."

"Yes, Your Honor," I said, retiring to pass the word.

There is no doubt that Justice Gallagher in his opinion in the *Coursolle* case for the most part followed and reiterated the prevailing law on the subject as it has been since the early days of the English common law. There is only one phase of it I don't quite go along with and that is the part where — really largely by way of dictum — he said in substance that the danger from the unshackling must be *here* and *now*.

In the light of Crazy Matt and men like him I think that under a proper showing and with careful jury instructions a man with a clear record of past violence and escape (regardless of the meekness of his present mien in court), and whether he is defendant or witness, might well remain under courtroom restraint, in extreme cases perhaps even while giving his testimony. To avoid unnecessary prejudice, such a violent witness or defendant might well be placed in the witness box (where his leg irons would be hidden) during the absence of the jury, which need never know about it.

Perry Mason mythology to the contrary, the courtroom is no place for idle bravado or for taking chances with violent histrionics of this kind. I *saw* what one bad actor did. Suppose he had instead attacked the defenseless and already failing judge? Any defendant who insists on calling a witness like Crazy Matt to testify for him might well be expected to share the risk that his man might have to be kept under physical restraint.

3
Attempting the Impossible

C AN a man be convicted of attempted murder if the gun
he uses is unloaded when he aims it and pulls the trigger?
This question is as loaded as the gun was not. The answer
depends apparently upon two things: upon the state of the
mind of the would-be marksman, and also upon the state of
the Union where the event took place.

The supreme court of Wisconsin recently had occasion to
grapple with this knotty problem under the following circumstances: Ralph Damms, aged thirty-three, and his wife, Mar-
jory, thirty-eight, had been separated; one morning he met
her on the street and prevailed upon her to get in his car and
go for a ride, during the course of which he referred darkly to
"judgment day" and how easy it was to die. Finally, he produced a semi-automatic pistol, which he aimed at his wife —
as she later testified — to show her he was "not kidding."
She was impressed. Still later they drove to a roadside restaurant, parked, and instead of eating sat in the car and quar-
reled.

Suddenly the wife got out of the car, shouted for help, and
started to run around the restaurant, with her husband in hot
pursuit. Then she slipped and fell, and as she later testified,
he caught up with her, and crouching at her side, held the

pistol to her head and pulled the trigger. But nothing happened; whereupon he shouted, "It won't fire! It won't fire!"

About the same time two traffic cops, who were inside the restaurant and heard the commotion, came barreling out and disarmed the husband, only to discover that his gun was unloaded. They later testified that they had seen the gun held at the wife's head when the husband pulled the trigger and that they had found the loaded clip and a box of cartridges back in the parked car.

That afternoon in the county jail the sheriff's men questioned the husband about his quixotic behavior. They said later that he told them he thought the gun was loaded. He was formally charged with attempted murder, hired himself some astute attorneys, pleaded innocent, and the case finally came up for trial.

At his trial the husband took the stand and testified that at the time he pulled the trigger the gun was pointed down at the ground and not at his wife's head; he denied that he had told the sheriff's deputies that he thought the gun was loaded; and he declared flatly that at the time of the tableau outside the restaurant he *knew* the pistol was unloaded. The various officers and the wife had already testified to the contrary, and the jury, after due deliberation, apparently took their word rather than the husband's: he was duly convicted of attempted murder and sentenced to state's prison.

The husband appealed his conviction to the supreme court of Wisconsin, his able attorneys arguing and citing numerous authorities to the effect that where, as here, it was utterly impossible to perform the act of murder because the gun was empty, there could be no valid conviction for any attempt at murder. They pointed out that there was no evidence that he had used the gun as a club. They argued that in all criminal attempt cases the intent and power to perform the intended act must conjoin, and that here they plainly didn't, and that moreover the evidence was insufficient to establish the requisite criminal intent to commit the act of murder and that therefore the trial court should have granted the defense motion for judgment notwithstanding the jury's verdict of guilty. As might be expected, the equally able prosecution attorneys, citing other authorities, argued quite to the contrary, adding further that anyway they thought it was rather bad public policy to let such unsocial and eccentric behavior go unpunished. What had he meant to do if not to kill her? was their argument in a nutshell.

In due course, Justice Currie delivered the opinion of the court, pointing out that Wisconsin possessed a statute defining criminal attempt as follows: "An attempt to commit a crime requires that the actor have an intent to perform acts and attain a result which, if accomplished, would constitute such crime and that he does acts toward the commission of the crime which demonstrate unequivocally, under all the circumstances, that he formed that intent and would commit the crime *except for the intervention of another person or some other extraneous facts.*" [italics added].

Conceding that there was considerable authority to the contrary, the judge went on to point out that the modern trend of the law in these attempt situations is to place the emphasis upon the dangerous propensities of the actor, as shown by his conduct, rather than upon how close he may have come to succeeding; and that this approach is more nearly in keeping with the large design of the criminal law to protect society and reform or restrain would-be offenders. In other words, he implied, the law punishes the demonstrated bad intent rather than splitting too-fine hairs over precisely what fortuitous events may have blocked its exercise.

Justice Currie pushed on in the rather dense Latinized prose so dear to the hearts of most judges, and which is due in part, at least, to the doleful fact that in the law it is frequently hard to say briefly that which needs also to be said accurately. "Sound public policy would seem to support the majority view that impossibility not apparent to the actor should not absolve him from the offense of attempt to commit the crime intended. An unequivocal act accompanied by intent should be sufficient to constitute a criminal attempt. Insofar as the actor knows, he has done everything necessary to insure the commission of the crime intended, and he should not escape punishment because of the fortuitous circumstance that by reason of some fact unknown to him it was impossible to effectuate the intended result." In summary, then, the good judge allowed that would-be criminals could not be saved by bungling their jobs.

His Honor wound up his opinion by holding that in his view there was sufficient evidence from which the jury could find beyond a reasonable doubt that the defendant intended to kill his wife and had indeed tried to. A majority of the court joined him in his affirmance of the defendant's conviction.

Only one lone voice was raised on behalf of the defendant's cause, that of Justice Dieterich dissenting, who pointed out that in his view the "other extraneous" factors mentioned in the quoted "attempt" statute must come from someone or something over which the actor himself had no control — such as a loaded gun misfiring or someone else having unloaded it — but that here the sole control of the admitted fact that the pistol was unloaded lay entirely with the defendant himself and not with any "extraneous" factor, which by definition must always come from without. For his part he would have freed the defendant on the semantics of the situation. He makes a rather persuasive point.

This interesting and curious case *(State v. Damms)* really deals with a triumph of a new philosophy of crime and punishment over the traditional semantic approach. The case is also reported in the *American Law Reports* and is followed by an exhaustive annotation exploring the various ramifications of this tricky subject, with cases both ways. The *ALR* article is far too long to digest here, but it is recommended that any spouse who feels an irresistible impulse to point an unloaded pistol at the head of his mate should first get and read it, carefully choosing his site before taking sight. Above all he should avoid indulging in "dry" target practice in the state of Wisconsin, where, as we have just seen, fruitless attempts to perform the impossible may still land one in prison.

4

The Shorn Lamb

THAT confession is good for the soul is one of those large resonant metaphysical propositions that are hard to prove, but that confessions of guilt are "good" for the solution of crime has been shown many times; there are thousands of men in prison and thousands of cases in the books to prove it. The confession of guilt is one of the oldest, swiftest, and most painless ways of clearing up crimes and disposing of criminals, and policemen, being as lazy and prideful as other men, long ago fell in love with it.

"Danny the Dip cracked last night, Mister D.A., and signed a full confession on the dotted line," is one of the sweetest and most exultant lines that can pass between police and public prosecutors. After all, it's pretty hard for the prosecution to lose a case where the defendant has in his own words told the jurors not only *that* he did it, but (as is usual in formally signed confessions) precisely how and why he did it. Even jurors possess a certain pride.

But to get a man to confess is one thing; to get his confession admitted in evidence at his court trial later is often quite another. For centuries in Anglo-American law the basic test of the admissibility at a trial of a previous confession of guilt is that it be voluntarily given; that is, that it be given without threats or duress or false promises. Hollywood myth peddlers to the contrary, all strong-arm methods are out — no racks, no castor oil, no rubber hoses, no hot foots, no third degrees, no beguiling inducements or promises.

The police rapidly got the message, and their resourcefulness over the years in wheedling confessions out of their recalcitrant charges without spoiling their later admissibility in court is some sort of a monument to Yankee ingenuity, if not precisely to Yankee morality. Police have used virtually every subterfuge under the sun to get their man to talk; if one can dream it they have probably done it.

What follows is a partial list of proven stratagems — field-tested, in the curious language of Madison Avenue — that police have used for years to get suspected or accused persons in their custody to confess their crimes. All are drawn from actual cases; virtually all the confessions thus obtained were later held properly admissible, even though the judge usually accompanied his ruling with a pained little lecture bewailing the naughty practices used by the police to obtain them.

One of the commonest and oldest dodges is pretending to have evidence not actually possessed — recovered loot, murder weapons, eyewitnesses, fingerprints. Another is pretending that the legal plight of the accused is not as bad as it actually is (telling the suspect, for example, that an actual murder victim has "recovered" and does not want to press charges). Another ruse is pretending that a missing accomplice has been caught and has confessed and incriminated the accused, the same strategy also being used on accomplices already in custody; or withholding vital information from the accused (a switch on faking facts, as above) that might otherwise cause him to remain silent. Thus, in one case, the police failed to tell the accused, who was being held for the removal and theft of some lengths of railroad track, that an engineer and fireman had been killed in a subsequent wreck, which of course made it a much graver offense.

I have just said that most judges admit confessions ob-

tained by trick while at the same time deploring the means
employed, usually delivering reproachful lectures on the subject, presumably to ease their troubled consciences. One case
was an exception: "Society and the criminal are at war,"
flatly declared one hard-boiled appellate judge in approving
the trial-court admission of a confession obtained by trick,
"and capture by surprise, or ambush, or masked battery is as
permissible in one case as in the other." If one is mildly
shocked by such language emanating from a state supreme
court, he should remember that judges are only men, and that
there are people among us, some in high places, who would
cheerfully revive the birch switch and the whipping post and
the rack without a pang.

Critics of this traditional distinction between barring confessions obtained by force while admitting those obtained by
guile frequently argue that the distinction is as illogical —
and as bad law — as it would be, say, to hold that to wrest a
man's purse from him by force is wrong but to swindle him
out of it is all right. "False analogy," the critics of these critics come back. "The main consideration in judging a confession is not so much the means used to extract it but the effect
that those means might have on the voluntariness and truth-
fulness of the confession thus obtained. The confession is the
thing. A truer analogy would be the distinction between gaining a woman's favor by force or gaining it by masculine wile;
the one is rape, which inspires only revulsion; the other is
seduction, which inspires only envy."

"Still 'tain't cricket," the critics of the distinction fight
back. "Men hired to represent the law should not break it in
order to enforce it. As Justice Brandeis once put it: 'Crime is
contagious. If the government becomes a lawbreaker, it invites every man to become a law unto himself; it invites anarchy.' "

"Sheer bleeding-heart nonsense," their opponents retort.
"Look, the true heart of the distinction is this: if you beat a
confession out of a man he may confess to anything he thinks

you want to hear simply to get you to stop beating him. This is what makes his confession involuntary and likewise untrustworthy. Look at all history down through Hitler and Stalin and beyond. But if you trick a confession out of him, that still does not make it any less voluntary and, since men rarely speak ill of themselves when they don't have to, is far more likely to be the truth."

All very devious, subtle and profound, you see. But back to more police stratagems.

Another means commonly used by police to fool a man into confessing his guilt is by disguising detectives and informers as fellow inmates or by using actual prisoners as stool pigeons. Evidently on the theory that it takes a thief to catch a thief, the detective may pose as the leader of a criminal gang and adroitly lead the envious suspect to apply for admission, thereafter quizzing the applicant on his past criminal record, presumably to prove his qualifications for admission to such an exclusive circle. "But what have you done lately?" or some variant is usually the payoff question. (In only one such case I have found was the confession later held bad and inadmissible; this on the ground that the confession of guilt thus obtained might well have been faked by the confessor simply to gain admission to the lodge, as it were, thus making it involuntary.)

Let's face it, criminals as a class, especially repeaters, are not among the brightest of mortals. Despite a persistent folklore to the contrary, the incidence of Ph.D.'s among them is woefully low; they are more often stupid, childishly emotional, and gullible almost beyond belief. And also pathetic. Thus, disguised detectives have obtained many a confession from contrite suspects by posing as stern come-to-Jesus revivalists ("Confession *is* good for the soul, my friend — come kneel with me") or by appealing to the crassest sort of superstition ("Look, boy, I'm a right good ol' monger doctor an' I kin work roots an' gummer folks an' git you clean off this here bad charge ag'in you. But firs' you got to admit your sins, so come now, boy, tell me what really happen").

Plain old-fashioned jailhouse eavesdropping has always been used, of course, but is rapidly giving way to the more insidious subtleties of the electronic age such as wiretapping, wired cells, hidden tape recorders, and diabolic devices that can augment even a whisper — the list is ever growing. (Modern decisions are stiffening considerably against the admission in any of our courts of incriminating evidence obtained electronically by means of any "physical trespass" on the privacy of a suspect in his home or place of business — this on a sort of "my-home-is-my-castle" theory — but this new concern has not yet been extended to persons languishing in jail.) Equally old-fashioned is the primitive device of intercepting and opening letters written by the accused, which last, far from exhausting the list of police stratagems, brings us down to a wily barber called Wilcox.

One guesses that barbering must be one of those callings most easily inducing a philosophical take-her-as-she-comes attitude among its practitioners. For barbers must minister cheerfully to the needs of everyone: to the good and the bad, the weak and the strong, the bald and the hirsute, the guilty and the innocent, even the quick and the dead. Barbers must also be prepared stoically to attend upon suspected murderers. Take the day Barber Wilcox visited Will Dunnigan in his cell in the county jail in Hillsdale, Michigan, ostensibly to cut his hair. (Though a man may be charged as a criminal, he is not required to defend himself looking like one.)

Two of Dunnigan's companions, Knox and Smith, were then being held in the same jail, but in different cells, awaiting trial on a charge of first-degree murder. The crime had allegedly been committed during a robbery. Will Dunnigan was being held on a minor charge unconnected with the murder, but the sheriff and his men suspected him of having taken part in it. When Barber Wilcox came to the jail to cut Will Dunnigan's hair, two of the sheriff's men arranged with him to get what information he could from the suspect Dunnigan and turn it over to them.

While the barber was shearing Dunnigan he prattled away, in the manner of barbers everywhere and eventually suggested to Dunnigan that if he wanted to communicate with his wife Nora, he, the barber, would be happy to deliver the message. The grateful Dunnigan fell in with the suggestion and rapidly scribbled a note which he handed the barber to give to his wife. Dunnigan now both figuratively and literally shorn, the canny barber quickly packed up his tools and left, on the way out delivering Dunnigan's letter to the sheriff. Barber Wilcox was practical as well as philosophical, you see — Will Dunnigans might come and go, but in the future there would doubtless be other uneasy heads to shear at the Hillsdale county jail. The letter read:

Dear Nora: I want to tell you something. If they ask you any questions, tell them that I got home at 12 o'clock, and if they ask you if I had a watch that night, tell them no, or no ring, if they should ask you, for I have told them that Walter Knox got the watch and ring, for I had to do it in order to clear myself, and I guess I can if you will help a little. It will mean five years for Walter Knox and life for Smith, and I don't know how much for myself. Now, don't forget to stick to what I have told you, will you, for it will help me a lot. Now, do as I have told you.

From Will.

On the strength of this letter Will Dunnigan was promptly charged with participation in the homicide with Knox and Smith, and wearing his new haircut, shortly appeared at his murder trial. There, through his lawyer, he objected strenuously to the admission into evidence of the damning letter offered by the prosecution, claiming that it was a privileged communication between husband and wife and was in any case obtained by trick and fraud. His objections were overruled, the letter was admitted, Will Dunnigan and his companions were convicted, and he was sentenced to serve life in Jackson Prison. He appealed to the Michigan supreme court, where in due course, after the usual arguments and briefs, Mr. Justice Brooke delivered the opinion of the court:

"An examination of the record leads us to believe that the letter was the principal if not the only tangible evidence against the accused," Justice Brooke began. "The importance of our ruling is therefore apparent." He then proceeded to demolish the appellant's claim that the letter was a privileged communication between man and wife. He did so on the ground that the communication had not yet been completed and that anyway Dunnigan had himself allowed the letter to fall into the hands of another.

He then turned his attention to the heart of the matter, namely, whether the letter was rendered inadmissible because it was obtained by trick and fraud. The question had never before been squarely presented in Michigan, and a man's freedom and whole future rode on the result. Meanwhile, Will Dunnigan's resourceful lawyers had dug up an old Michigan case in which the following language occurred: "But they [confessions] must be voluntary, and without any influence being exerted by the officer, either of threats, promises, artifice, or duress."

Justice Brooke met this disturbing dictum head on. "This declaration . . . does not accurately state the law," His Honor declared. ". . . The true reason for the exclusion of involuntary confessions — that is, those obtained by improper threats or promises — is that, because of such threats or promises the accused is led to believe that it is for his interest to make a confession, regardless of its truth or falsity.

"The use of artifice, trickery, or fraud in inducing a confession will not alone render such confession inadmissible," he continued. "If the artifice used involved a promise tending to induce a false confession, it would operate to exclude, not because of the trick, but because, by use of the trick . . . an untrue confession had been secured. . . ."

Here I might pause and interpolate that, while all jurisdictions hold that to be admissible in evidence a confession of guilt must be voluntary, poor Will Dunnigan found himself in a bind. If he claimed on his appeal, as he might have, that his letter to his wife was merely an admission rather than a full confession of guilt, he would run smack into the rule then prevailing in most states (although our federal courts have recently cast doubt on it) that admissions are usually not subject to the same rigorous restrictions on admissibility as are confessions. If on the other hand he conceded that his letter was indeed a full confession of guilt, then his goose was cooked if his argument against admissibility failed. Will Dunnigan chose the latter course and so we are back again to Mr. Justice Brooke:

"Applying these principles to the case under consideration," he droned on, "it is apparent that the promise of Wilcox [the barber] to carry a letter from the respondent to his wife could in no manner . . . induce him falsely to admit his guilt. . . . The letter was written by respondent himself, and it does not appear that its contents were suggested by Wilcox or any other person."

While it was growing abundantly plain that Will Dunnigan had gambled and lost, His Honor paused to deliver the traditional pained little lecture to the police, all, I may add, in traditional, fine, taut cliché-haunted judicial rhetoric:

"While we feel constrained to hold that the learned circuit judge did not err in admitting the document, we do not wish to be understood as setting the seal of our approval upon the methods used in securing it. Those methods were distinctly reprehensible. The presumption of innocence surrounds all persons charged with the commission of crime, and it is the duty of those charged with the custody and prosecution of such persons to treat them with fairness in order that the in-

nocent may thereby be protected, and the guilty convicted
and punished. When such a course is followed, the dignity of
the law is upheld and its administration is, as it should be,
above criticism."

His lecture over, the purged justice swiftly delivered his
decision. "The conviction must be affirmed," he declared.
Will Dunnigan had been shorn again.

There is little doubt that the decision in Dunnigan was
sound law when it was reached — or at least the prevailing
law — and that it has been followed by most American
courts virtually down to the present day. But in recent years
there have been increasing rumblings of discontent with the
notion that the officers of our courts of justice can legiti-
mately trick a person into confessing crime, that they can in
effect break one kind of law — the moral — while seeking to
enforce another — the criminal.

Most of these rumblings have come from our federal
courts, and indeed in at least one case the U.S. Supreme
Court dumped a state court murder conviction in which a
confession obtained by fraud and trick had been admitted,
though evidently not in sweeping enough terms to banish the
practice. In this rather unpublicized 1961 decision the Court
said bluntly that whether or not the confession thus obtained
was true was entirely irrelevant; that the real question was
whether it was "freely self-determined." Change was clearly
in the wind.

Suddenly in 1964 these rumblings burst into full judicial
eruption; succor came abruptly to deceived confessors, if
rather obliquely. It came with the U.S. Supreme Court's
precedent-shattering decision in the *Escobedo* case. That case
did not involve a confession obtained by trick, but rather the
larger right of an accused person (or, more accurately, an
about-to-be-accused person) to see his lawyer before making
an admission or a confession of any kind. The decision was a
disturbing and reverberant one, and it would doubtless take a

whole book to discuss properly, let alone dissect, all its mean-
ings and subtle overtones. Lawyers and legal scholars, not to
mention judges, cops, and prosecutors, are still grappling with
its implications.

For now it is enough to say that the decision holds that, at
least from now on, any suspect against whom an investigation
has reached an "accusatory stage" (and by necessary implication any formally accused person) is entitled to see his lawyer, if he has one, before confessing or else the confession is
inadmissible in any court in the land.

Court decisions do carry implications; they do tend to reverberate. This is so because not only are they decided upon
principles but sometimes — especially on the U.S. Supreme
Court in constitutional cases — they either enunciate new
principles or give new applications to old principles that carry
their doctrine far beyond their particular facts. Thus with the
decision in *Escobedo*. It not only decided a specific question
in a specific case upon specific facts — namely, that where a
prime suspect in police custody is denied the chance to see his
retained lawyer before confessing, his confession is no good
— but, according to many views, did so in such a way and
depending upon such broad principles that it *seems* also necessarily to embrace the following propositions:

1. If such a suspect lacks a lawyer but asks for one his
request must be granted on pain of throwing out any later
confession he makes without one.

2. If a suspect hasn't got a lawyer or if he fails to ask for
one, the police must first warn him of his right to see one and
provide one for him if he wants one and can't afford it, or any
confession he makes is likewise bad and inadmissible.

It is this last implication of the case that has perhaps raised
the greatest storm of controversy and, as with all pioneering
landmark decisions (witness the continuing tempest over the
historic "one-man-one-vote" reapportionment case), it will
probably take a series of supplemental decisions to hammer
out any lingering uncertainties on the harsh anvil of experi-

ence. Indeed, a whole flock of such related cases is now pending before the Supreme Court.

Since the foregoing was written, the Supreme Court has indeed gone whole hog; in a recent series of cases culminating in *Miranda v. Arizona* it flatly held and laid down that henceforth the police may not even question, much less obtain an admissible confession from, a person in custody until he has first been told that he has a right to remain silent, that anything he says may be used against him, and that he has a right to consult a lawyer; that if he should wish to consult a lawyer the interrogation must stop until his lawyer shows up or, if he is unable to retain one, until a lawyer has been provided him; and, lastly, that if the police nevertheless continue questioning him without the presence of a lawyer — on a theory that he has been duly warned, proffered a lawyer, and has waived these rights — and a statement is taken, "a heavy burden rests on the [prosecution] . . . to demonstrate that the defendant knowingly and intelligently waived" his proffered rights.

These last blunt words quoted from *Miranda* will doubtless revolutionize future police practice on questioning persons in custody. It will because it must, since for all practical purposes the only confessions of crime that will henceforth be admissible in any court will be those made after warning, proffer of counsel, and waiver. Why? Because if the man clams up there is of course no confession, and if he consults a lawyer there will quite likely be no confession.

This last is so because under our adversary system of litigation it is the job of a lawyer to do the best he can do for his man, regardless of his guilt or innocence — and advising him to make a police confession of guilt is not normally the best prelude to effective representation. Hence any lawyer worth his salt will doubtless tell his man to clam up in order either to get him off entirely or to improve his later bargaining position to get a reduced charge or sentence. (In other words, a savvy lawyer is far more apt to "cop him out" — that is, plead him guilty — in court much later in the case than to disarm his man by confession at the very start.) So the real pinch comes when the suspect has been warned and offered a lawyer and nevertheless still says he wants to talk — "spill his guts," in the refined parlance of the police. It is here that the police must drastically change their ways. I have some ideas on the possible trend of that change.

If, heaven forbid, I were still a district attorney, I do not think I would spend my time, as so many seem to do these days, in fretting and fuming over the new decisions or in trying to overrule the U. S. Supreme Court, at best an unproductive if not paranoid pastime. Instead I think I would round up all the cops in my county, light up the cigars, and explain the new decisions and their implications in great detail. After that the dialogue might run something like this:

"Hell, we might as well give the country back to the Indians. We'll never convict anyone now — not even a common drunk."

To this I might reply, "You sound like the aggrieved police chief out West who greeted *Miranda* with these deathless words: 'It's the damndest thing I ever heard of — we may as well close up shop.' But you are both wrong."

"Why?"

"Because confessions, however important, are only *one* way to convict persons accused of crime. The Supreme Court has not banished the use of confessions in criminal cases but simply laid down stricter ground rules for their admissibility. And anyway, most careful and fair-minded cops and prosecutors — ahem, like us — have already been quietly following substantially these same requirements for years, with the possible exception of proffering a lawyer to indigent suspects."

"But a lawyer in *every* case! Gawd!"

"Again wrong. It does *not* mean a lawyer in every case. It simply means that if you choose to *question* the guy, you've first got to offer him a lawyer, which he may waive. While I don't downgrade the efficacy of a confession in cracking a criminal case, in many if not most of your cases you don't need one and shouldn't ask for one. Too often 'taking a confession' has got to be a lazy man's way of doing your work."

"But supposing we do want to question him and he takes a free lawyer?"

"What's wrong with that? Isn't the poor lone bastard in your clutches who cannot afford a lawyer precisely the guy who most needs one when the chips are down? And after *Escobedo,* what was the Supreme Court going to do? Don't you see? Any other rule would have favored the well-heeled professional hoodlum, the gangster, the mobster, the rich bitch, the fat cat — the very people least in need of impromptu police lectures about their rights. Most of *them* could tell you. . . . But what I'm talking about now is the guy who waives lawyers, rights, everything, and still wants to talk — the only confession situation that really counts anymore. There has simply got to be a new deal on that."

"What are you getting at, man?"

"I'm getting at this, Mac. That we've got to change our ways, get with it, lean over backwards, and from now on exceed even *Escobedo,* out-*Miranda Miranda.*"

"Riddles, riddles! Cut out the foggy lawyer talk and say what you mean."

"Okay, you asked for it. From now on you've got to take your confessions — all of them — out of the jailhouse and away from the detective-sergeant's cubbyhole."

"Why?"

"I just told you why. Because all future confessions taken the old way will come into court with two strikes against them and batting the third under a heavy cloud of suspicion."

"Why suspicion?"

"Because that's what the words 'heavy burden' used in the *Miranda* case really mean. They mean that all 'waived' confessions taken the old way will now be viewed with frank judicial skepticism."

"But we've always taken our confessions the old way."

"That's what's got to change. Look, what have you got to hide? If one lone man in custody is willing to confess his sins to the world — which is the effect of his confession once it's admitted in court — why should you continue to insist that he *first* tell only you? If he has nothing to hide, why should you?"

"Do we now take the man out on the street corner and summon a crowd of gawkers to come watch him spill his guts?"

"You're getting warm. All of which brings me to my plan."

"What plan?"

"I'm still working on it and I haven't thought it all out yet and it may require an act of the legislature and involve a wee Constitutional question, but —"

"Cut the doubletalk and let's have it."

"Okay. I'll give you just the highlights. You've got a guy in custody suspected, say, of murder. You warn him of his rights and offer him a lawyer, but he says he 'don't want no bloody mout'piece' and he still wants to talk."

"So naturally we quick take his confession while he's hot."

"Dead wrong. Instead, under my plan, you quick take him before a sort of revolving Confession Commission composed of outstanding lawyers, retired judges, and other citizens of impeccable rectitude —"

"I love that *other* citizens. You cool lawyers!"

"Don't interrupt. You take him before this Confession Commission where he is carefully *rewarned* of all his rights and again offered a lawyer — the whole bit — and, if he still waives everything, for the *first* time his confession is taken, everything being recorded on sound movies. Maybe even in color."

"But wouldn't that mean everything would be spilled in the newspapers — which we've never done before — and that way maybe queer the case for illegal publicity and certainly tip off his pals?"

"I didn't say that the proceedings before the Confession Commission should be public. I say only that confessions should no longer be taken in the anonymous one-sided privacy of the station house. A confession, like a judge, should not only *be* right but *look* right. Don't you see? It's your way of shouldering the new policeman's 'burden' imposed by *Miranda*."

"Does this new-fangled Confession Commission of yours take any part in the proceedings?"

"Yes, at least to the extent of assuring itself that the confessor definitely knows and understands his rights, is not laboring under fear or duress, really doesn't want a lawyer, and indeed wants to spill his story. Don't you see? All this is calculated to meet head on the 'heavy burden' imposed by *Miranda* and to discourage any possible future contention by the confessor that he had not 'knowingly and intelligently' waived his rights. In other words, from now on you stamp all your confessions with a blue-ribbon seal of authenticity."

"All this sounds damned cumbersome and expensive."

"Granted, but is it not small compared with the expense and turmoil and uncertainty of a subsequent appeal by the confessor, maybe clear to Washington, frequently made many years later, after many of you guys have retired and opened your taverns, or witnesses have died or moved away, and literarily inclined district attorneys have turned from splitting hairs to splitting infinitives?"

Where does all this leave poor Will Dunnigan, patiently waiting in the wings during this long digression? What's in it for him? Will *Escobedo* and *Miranda* magically spring him from prison if he is still alive? The answer, bluntly, is No. At the same term of Court in which *Miranda* was handed down, the Court also held that the "new" rules on questioning suspects are not retroactive. So once again Will Dunnigan is shorn.

If Will had written his Nora yesterday, he would doubtless

now go free on any subsequent appeal. But he was over fifty years too early for the new dispensation. There is also little doubt that the new rules will put a decided crimp in most if not all future confessions obtained by fraud.

For one thing, how do you go about tricking a man into confessing his guilt in front of a savvy criminal lawyer? But, more practically, clever police deceivers who would continue to pose as pals or fellow inmates or benevolent "git-you-free" witch doctors or forgiving father-confessors or heaven knows what else in order to soften up their charges are likely to give the whole show away if it falls out that they must henceforth preface their little acts of false camaraderie or whatever by first soberly warning their prospective pigeons about their rights to counsel.

The two roles simply don't go together, don't "play," as theater folk might say, and one suspects that if Barber Wilcox had tried it with Will Dunnigan he might have emerged from the cell not with an incriminating letter to Will's Nora but with a rather close haircut of his own. Meanwhile an obscure modern Samson, Will Dunnigan — if he is still alive and un-paroled — has languished an appalling number of years in state's prison.

5

O Land of Fun and Games —
and Happy Litigation

NEVADA is that happy land where one can get parted from one's money or one's mate with equal ease. There is only one fly in the ointment: anyone staying there a full six weeks (the length of residence required to get a divorce) runs some risk of getting muscle-bound yanking away at all those slot machines. But there are other cultural diversions in this resourceful land of eternal fun; one can even take a chance playing golf. George Gibson did.

One of the many clubs in the state offered to pay $5,000 to any person who shot a hole in one on the local golf course, provided he paid fifty cents for the attempt. Many aspirants had paid and failed, but the undaunted Gibson paid his four bits and stepped up and, as golfers sometimes do, eyed the distant green and then the ball and — WHAM — the bloody thing soared, landed, and believe it or not, rolled right into the cup! One could have knocked him over with a number two iron.

Modestly dusting his nails on his shirt front, George stepped away and inquired politely where he should go to collect that five grand he had just won. "Go get lost," was the substance of the withering reply he got. Being a man of character and determination (and normal cupidity), he instead hired a smart Las Vegas lawyer and sued the recalcitrant fun club for his five grand plus costs and interest. In the trial court he won, and the aggrieved club appealed to the supreme court of Nevada.

There the club plaintively argued it should not have to pay for two reasons: one, that the deal they offered was an illegal wagering contract and therefore unenforceable in any court of law; and two, that the trial judge below was dead wrong in holding, as he had, that shooting a "hole in one" is a feat of skill and not a pure matter of chance. Mr. Justice McNamee delivered the court's opinion. At the outset he agreed with the club that while licensed gambling was legal in Nevada, the courts could not be used to collect money won in gambling — which is the prevailing rule throughout the country (besides being a nice handy break for the impoverished gambling gentry of Nevada). It therefore first became necessary for the court to determine whether the deal was a gambling contest, he said, and he got on with that chore:

"It is generally held . . . that the offer of a prize to a contestant . . . who performs a specified act is not invalid as being . . . gambling. . . . The offer by one party of specified compensation for the performance of a certain act as a proposition to all persons who may accept and comply with its conditions constitutes a promise by the offeror [the club here]. The performance of that act is the consideration for such promise. The result is an enforceable contract."

He next explained the difference between a prize, which is legal, and a bet, which is not: "in the former the person offering the same has no chance of gaining back the thing offered but . . . must lose; . . . in the latter each party . . . has a chance of gain and takes a risk of loss. . . ." He quoted from an old Indiana case: " 'In a . . . bet there must be two parties . . . who must either lose or win. In a . . . [prize] there is but one [who can win or lose]. A [prize] is a reward

. . . for some act done; a wager is a stake upon some uncertain event. In a premium [legalese for "prize"] it is known who is to give before the event; in a wager it is not known until after the event.' "

Justice McNamee pressed on with his enlightening lecture: "The fact that each contestant is required to pay an entrance fee where [it] . . . does not specifically make up the purse . . . does not convert the contest into a wager. . . ." He then declared that the "hole-in-one" offer was a valid and enforceable contract, and next turned to the argument of the appellant golf club that the trial judge had goofed in finding that the plaintiff's feat in sinking the golf ball in one stroke was, in effect, skill rather than bull-headed luck.

He answered this argument by simply saying that since the basic offer was not a wager it no longer mattered, noting in passing, however, that the plaintiff Gibson had anyway produced an expert witness, a golf pro called Capps who, though conceding that luck is always a factor in such a feat, added that "a skilled player will get . . . [the ball] in the area where luck will take over more often than an unskilled player."

McNamee, J., was rapidly nearing the eighteenth hole. "The test of the character of a game is not whether it contains an element of chance or an element of skill, but which is the dominant element. . . . It was within the province of the trial court to determine this question. . . . Affirmed."

George Gibson had now also shot himself a legal hole-in-one and won his case. The report regrettably does not reveal whether or not His Honor played golf.

As Justice McNamee has just indicated, once you win a contest there remains the business of collecting the prize, and some of the sponsors don't pay; from the number of cases on the subject quite a few of them don't, in fact. So if you win and have to sue to collect, you've first got to show that the basic deal isn't illegal to begin with, that you've got a valid enforceable contract, and finally that you've done your part under it. If the thing is illegal to begin with you're out in the cold from the start.

Now to some refinements.

Nevada is not the only land of fun and games; one suspects from the wealth of cases that the whole blooming country is infected with a passion for prize-winning contests. In fact I'll bet my favorite fly rod against anything you want (see what a sport I am — I can't possibly lose even if you win, 'cause it's an unenforceable bet, see?) that one day, when our two-headed descendants gather courage enough to prowl through the rubble that was once our Republic, they will conclude to a man that as a people we spent a third of our time crouched hypnotized before our television sets swilling beer, another third entering and toiling over prize contests or watching others hard at it, and the remaining third driving madly about the countryside hurling empty beer cans left and right. Meanwhile let's look more closely at these curious contests, and at some of the curious litigation they have spawned.

Back in 1912 the publisher of the Asbury Park *Journal* in New Jersey generously offered a brand new automobile to the baby receiving the most votes in the upcoming baby parade. Each new subscription entitled the subscriber to the *Journal* for one year and — there was more, there always is — to a coupon worth 500 votes in the baby contest. The plaintiff, a proud father, stoically shelled out $750 for 75,000 votes, all of which he promptly voted for his own pride and joy. Alas, when all the damp diapers were cleared away his urchin had lost.

The smarting father then insisted that the *Journal* prepare to deliver him its paper for the next 150 years. (Let's see, 1912 plus 150 — that would take him to the year 2062!) The *Journal* refused to deliver him any paper at all, saying the whole scheme was an illegal gamble which the father had ungraciously lost. The father went to court and won before a jury. The paper appealed, and this towering question in jurisprudence got to New Jersey's highest court, which affirmed, thus giving the father, if he survives his subscription, a kind of dubious form of immortality. One wistfully wonders whether there still *is* an Asbury Park *Journal*. Yet the same year in Georgia an equally dogged subscriber lost under much the same circumstances.

Speaking of baby parades fills me with a weepy nostalgia — "O lost, O grieved" — and drives me helplessly to a digression about the first time I ran for district attorney, this against a personable young fellow lawyer equally gnawed by the gnat of ambition. That autumn the neighboring iron-mining town of Hematite was holding a gala Fall Festival and Baby Parade and I wondered just how I could convert this deathless affair into an irresistible countywide itch to elect Traver prosecutor. It was a problem. Now I never did learn precisely what the Fall Festival was all about (the sponsoring merchants seemed far more concerned with the flutter of dollar bills than with falling leaves), but I doubt I shall ever forget that Baby Parade.

The three-day festival was to be concluded by a free-for-all procession of prize-seeking offspring entered from all over the county. The masterminds of the festival shrewdly guessed that no baby parade could possibly ever miss, based as it was upon the sound psychology that even the most leaky and evil-looking brat is regarded as a picture of matchless charm and beauty by its adoring parents. For days I pondered a way to get in on the act. Then the day before the parade, while campaigning in a Hematite tavern — by then I was drawing the line nowhere — I ran across Big Buller Beaudin, a three-hundred-pound local slave to Old Cordwood, my bailiwick's favorite blended whiskey.

"Look," rotund Buller said as I dubiously handed him my cards and matches. "I'm awful sick today. Terrible hangover. Think I'm gonna die. Gimme a quarter an' I'll vote for you twice."

In his travail Buller drew his lips up into a moist rosebud pout and blew out his enormously fat pink cheeks. At that moment he looked like an unfortunate cherub whose thyroid had run amok. Then the inspiration hit me and I suddenly pictured plump Buller in a nightgown and a ruffled baby's cap . . .

"Look, Buller," I said, my voice suddenly grown hoarse with animal cunning, "how'd you like to make yourself ten bucks instead?"

"What doin'?" Buller said, rallying swiftly.

"Just sitting on your fat prat and riding in the big parade tomorrow."

"You mean the baby parade?"

"Sure, sure, Buller," I mollified him, dangling more bait. "All you got to do is sit there and fork down a fifth of Old Cordwood. Nobody'll ever recognize you."

"Hm," Buller mused, pondering my offer as my mind raced. Let's see: I'd rent an old carriage — the kind with wavy fringe on top — and one of those ancient donkeys (the symbol of my party) from McVannel's Livery Stable, hitch the donkey to the carriage, install Big Baby Buller and his bottle of Old Cordwood in the carriage, drape "Traver for D.A." signs from the carriage and over the donkey's back — and let the people laugh me into the district attorneyship. "Hm . . ." went Buller, rocking thoughtfully.

"Of course if you don't *want* the ten bucks and the free fifth . . ." I turned as though to go.

"Don't be hasty!" Buller shrilled in terror. "I'll do it! I — I was jest gettin' up my courage to hit you fer five bucks on account."

"Nothing at all, Buller," I said, airily whipping five dollars off the roll of six I happened to be carrying. "I'll meet you right here at ten tomorrow morning. The parade starts at eleven. I'll have everything ready — even to the diaper!"

"Okay, okay," Buller said, snatching the five dollars from me with eager trembling hands. "Ten o'clock here tomorrow — sharp on the dot."

"Okay, Buller," I said, and away I darted, filled with dazzling plans for rented donkeys, carriages, baby clothes, bottles of Old Cordwood, and irresistible political slogans.

Sharp at ten the next morning one of McVannel's drivers and I carefully threaded our way across Iron Street, guiding the bored donkey through a maze of baby buggies and their weeping passengers to the rear of Torreano's Tavern, there to pick up Buller Beaudin and dress him in swaddling clothes. "Whoa!" said the driver to the disconsolate donkey.

"Wait out here, Fred," I told the driver, leaping gaily from the carriage with my satchel of props and darting into the tavern's family entrance. "Hello, Joe," I hailed the proprietor. "Where's Big Buller Beaudin?"

Joe shook his head and led me to the back card room, switching on the single flyblown overhead bulb. "There's your Buller. If you can find enough help, I'd be much obliged if you'd move him."

There was an inert Buller, half sitting and half sprawled across the billiard-green card table, out like a light. "Buller!" I shouted. I shook him wildly. "Wake up, Buller! The parade starts in forty minutes!" Vast Buller just rolled from side to side as I shook him and then came back to rest, like a huge soft gyroscopic toy. "Blub wah," he muttered, in a kind of rumbling five-dollar burp.

There I was, out all my money — the rental of the donkey and the driver and livery equipment and all my expensive props and I had no baby! "Joe," I murmured, turning white-faced to the proprietor. "Before I try moving this alcoholic slob — or delivering a baby of my own — would you please kindly bring me a double shot of Old Cordwood? I — I need a drink awful bad!"

"Blub wah," Buller said again, rallying a bit at the magical mention of his favorite brand. The effort was too much for him; he began to snore. I shut my glazed eyes and wagged my head and sank to a chair beside him.

The baby parade went off on schedule. At eleven sharp the mayor's attendants hoisted him up on his horse and steadied him there, the Hematite American Legion band burst into a jazzed-up version of Brahms' "Lullaby" — and away rolled several hundred moist, squalling, and unhappy infants pushed by an equal number of anxious and perspiring mothers. At the very end of the parade, drawn by a donkey, rode the biggest, fattest, and wettest baby of all — laughing, bawling, cooing, gurgling, hiccuping, burping, daintily patting his damp bangs — all the while beatifically sluicing down a bottle of Old Cordwood through a red rubber nipple.

The huge baby occasionally paused and, like a princeling bestowing largess, carelessly flung a handful of campaign matches to a scrambling and grateful populace. In all the excitement and jollity nobody noticed that the baby's nightshirt was stuffed with wine straw and old newspapers and that his cheeks were distended with huge wads of tinfoil. In fact, to this day nobody but good old Joe Torreano and McVannel's driver knew that this baby — who incidentally won a special prize — was none other than the spindly candidate for D.A. himself.

The election came and went. I was elected. My wife wept.

Many if not most prize contests never get in the courts at all because so many of them are patently illegal lotteries, which include virtually all raffles, drawings, door prizes, bingo, bank nights, and the like. I should know because as a former politician who had periodically to run for district attorney I perforce bought hundreds of raffle tickets on most of these things and more. Stout is my belief that I shall never go to hell: I've helped shingle too many churches. The main reason I lack a share in a synagogue is that in my day we hadn't any. It seemed that every time a church shingled a roof or installed a new grate or hung a new bell the congregation fanned out like locusts amongst us politicians and administered The Bite. "How many tickets can we put you down for, Mr. Traver?" they would leer. "We've always voted for you, you know." Invariably I was putty in their hands.

During my time as prosecutor, although I cracked down hard on all forms of public commercial gambling, I always closed my eyes to "church" gambling, including bingo. There is no warrant in the law for making this distinction and it is a lovely example of the prosecutor as legislator. I guess I must have reflected that occasionally the Devil has to be beaten by his own tail. . . .

I estimate I could have roofed Notre Dame Cathedral with all the church raffle tickets I bought during my time as D.A. Once I was unlucky enough to win a new broiler containing a dead turkey, and I had to act awful fast to decline it in time for a reraffle. It had simply never occurred to me that anyone might ever *win* one of these things. After that I bought all my raffle tickets in the name of my daughter Julie, but the charm was broken — she never won.

The books are full of jolly lawsuits against newspapers involving prize contests to stimulate advertising or circulation. Many also involve suits against churches, stores, and especially, in the older cases, piano companies. The gimmicks are endless and, to name but a few, have involved guessing the outcome of presidential and other elections and engaging in such soaring cerebral flights as counting black dots in an ad or guessing the number of beans in a bottle. Then there are endless puzzles and word games and choosing a name for a new product or tavern or townsite or subdivision. (There is often some attempt to inject enough skill into the thing to keep the element of luck at least arguable.) Quite a few of these cases involve suits by contractors and architects who have submitted plans in contests for proposed new buildings. (I was charmed to discover that, fittingly enough, the old Cook County courthouse in Chicago was born out of such lovely litigation, but the case is too dreary to go into, so I'll skip it.)

Promoters have done just about everything one can imagine to avoid keeping their word and paying as promised, such as changing the rules in mid-course, rigging the results, conspiring with certain favored contestants, "reaching" the judges, in a pinch even calling the contest off — and, of course, in court contritely defending on the lofty moral ground that now for the first time they suddenly realize the thing they had publicly sponsored was an illegal gamble. Prizes have ranged from money (the prime favorite) to autos to ponies to cultural trips to Florida or Disneyland; from houses to empty lots to public weddings — ad infinitum.

Quite a few of these cases have been defended successfully on the grounds that the scheme was indeed an illegal bet or a lottery, as noted, but there is evidence that many judges lean over backwards to nail greedy promoters who renege on their promises. The general swinishness of this whole world of contests and prizes isn't reserved to promoters alone, however; many of the contestants are just as bad, and they have employed every trick in the book, even to bribing employees of the promoters, to gain an unfair advantage over their fellow contestants. Often they fight among themselves, and an inspiring sight it is, something like watching a pack of jackals snarling over a bone.

In a wry Utah case two married couples drove together to a Labor Day wingding in the plaintiff husband's car. The defendant husband paid the entrance fee, for which he was given six tickets to a drawing on an automobile. Before the drawing the two men laughingly agreed to share equally if they won, ho, ho, ho! The defendant won the car but surprisingly "forgot" his agreement to share. The plaintiff sued, won in lower court, but lost on appeal because the basic plan was held to be a lottery. Thus ended a beautiful friendship between these lovely people.

In a more recent Kentucky case the plaintiff had earlier purchased chances on a new car to be raffled at a labor union picnic. On the day of the big picnic he found he had to work, so he cagily initialed the tickets and gave them to a girlfriend to attend in his place, promising her twenty-five dollars if he won. Naturally his ticket won, but she conveniently forgot her promise and kept the car. The plaintiff sued and won, despite the contention of the *ex*-girlfriend that the deal was a raffle and an illegal gamble which the courts shouldn't enforce. On her appeal, the higher court, confronted with this profound judicial poser, held that since their own side agreement was a legal agency contract, separate from the admittedly illegal drawing itself, the plaintiff should prevail. Since then there have been other cases to the same effect.

One comes away from reading these squalid cases somehow wanting to gargle and take a shower. It isn't only the dreary exhibition of greed and lack of pride and general pettiness these cases so eloquently exhibit, bad as that is, but one's own sense of wonder and dismay at how incredibly *cheaply* so many people will eagerly sell out not only their friends, but themselves, their honor, their self-respect. But enough of prize contests and fun and games; I have suddenly grown weary of the whole thing.

6

Hypnotism:
Mysterious Stepchild of Medicine

ONE summer when I was a boy I used to stand for hours before the window of a local furniture store. In this window was a large bed, and in this bed lay a resolutely sleeping man, nightcap and all, who, a large placard told the beholder, had recently been hypnotized by Hadrian the Hypnotist, then doing a land-office business on the stage over at Ed Butler's old Opera House. The gimmick was that anyone who could guess the closest moment when the sleeper would awake would win a handsome bedroom suite or something equally elegant. (Even I surmised that the awakening would doubtless have to be before the great Hadrian finished his local stint and left town.)

Certainly the sleeping man must have been awfully tired, because day after day I used to go down to Gately's store to check his slumbers. Under my beady surveillance, he never once moved or batted an eye — even when I slyly tapped suddenly on his window with my trusty jackknife. Day after day I was held there as in a fiend's clutch, fascinated and sorely puzzled. He never moved.

"But how does he go to the bathroom?" I one day asked my mother after returning from my vigil.

"I don't know, son. Maybe he doesn't," she replied.

"But everybody does," I insisted.

"Maybe he goes at night."

"No, Mama, Leo and his pals stayed up way late last Saturday night to catch him at it, but he never got up or moved all night." Leo was an emancipated older brother who could occasionally stay out late.

"Then I really don't know, son. Maybe he doesn't have to."

"But everybody has to. What is this hypnotism thing, Mama?"

"They put you in a trance."

"Who does? And what is a trance, Mama?"

"It — it's — oh dear me — it's where they — somebody who knows how to — by the power of suggestion deprives you of your will. You — you are mesmerized."

"What's mesmerized, Mama?"

With the back of her hand my mother wearily brushed some stray wisps of hair off her forehead. "Please go bounce your ball off the roof, son, or I'll *never* get these pasties in the oven in time for supper. Now please run along."

"Yes, Mama."

The sleeping man has been long gone out of Gately's window; in fact Gately's old store is also gone (they moved farther down Main Street), long ago replaced by a gas station. But I am still puzzled by hypnosis, as many people are, who tend to regard it as a baffling form of magic. My dictionary, if anything, only increases my boyhood puzzlement:

"The induction of a state resembling sleep or somnambulism," it says, "differing from it especially in a greater rapidity of pulse and respiration. . . . and in extreme suggestibility. . . . Normally the person . . . does not remember what has occurred during the sleep. . . . [It] is induced

either physiologically . . . or by suggestion, ordinarily operative only on a willing patient. . . . There are degrees
. . . characterized as lethargic, cataleptic and somnambulis-
tic. . . ."

I turn to my encyclopedia: *"Hypnotism,* Braid's term
(1842) for animal magnetism or mesmerism (see Mesmer).
It is induced in a relaxed subject by monotonous repetition of
words and gestures . . . [and] some people are not affected.
. . . [In] deep hypnosis, sensory system and muscles are
affected, supernormal feats cause no fatigue [and] are forgotten. Briefly used by Freud in psychoanalysis, it is still used
in some therapy and in study of mental activities."

Obediently I see Mesmer, as directed, and am disarmed to
note in three lines that Mesmer was a German physician who
was born in 1733 and died in 1815 and "developed a system
of treatment through hypnotism called mesmerism (see Hypnotism)." Having come full circle I sigh and go mix a drink,
being a little big now to go bounce my ball off the roof. But I
am still puzzled by hypnotism, a puzzlement I seem to share
with many courts.

Several years ago in Houston the following ad appeared in
the local paper, spelling, punctuation, and all:

"DO YOU FEEL AFRAID and don't know why? Do you feel
insecure? Do you feel inferior around people and cannot
make decisions? Do you have tension? Nervousness? Do you
have a compulsive habit like drinking or smoking or overeat-
ing? Do you think the worst and not the best? Do you dread
new situations? Do you have to push yourself to do your
work? Have you tried everything? You haven't tried Hypnosis. Over 600 have recovered from these problems Perma-
nently! Call now for a private interview without cost or obligation. Free Lecture. Roy Masters, Director of Institute of
Hypnosis, will demonstrate his recently discovered technique
— 7:30 every Thursday evening . . . You Are Invited —

Without Obligation!" This ad was accompanied by a picture of the hypnotist, Roy Masters.

The paper shortly ran a second ad by Mr. Masters, which included a picture of the master touching the hand of a smiling dark young woman: "Hypnotized Through Interpreter — Esther Alvarez, a Spanish orphan who for 16 years lived in the unbearable misery of blackouts, vomiting and morbid fears, her skin was too painful to touch and she could not hold a job . . . Today Esther is well and working. Hypnosis has given her a chance to live — along with over 300 others this year. For Esther it took seven visits (this is average). Successful cases are permanent without further need for hypnosis . . ." Then followed a partial repetition of the first ad, concluding with Mr. Masters's name and address and the time of his next lecture.

A skeptic called Libby attended one of these lectures and later submitted to a treatment — and then ungratefully signed a criminal complaint against Roy Masters for unlawfully practicing medicine without a license contrary to a Texas statute that broadly and in part defines a medical practioner as one "who shall diagnose, treat or offer to treat any disease or disorder, mental or physical . . . by any system or method, or to effect cures thereof and charge . . . money . . . [for doing so]."

Roy Masters indignantly denied the charge and at his trial the complainant Libby unmasked himself as an undercover investigator for the Houston Better Business Bureau, testifying substantially as follows: That he attended one of the lectures along with about twenty other people; that Roy Masters spoke to them about several of his cases, including his success with Esther Alvarez, the girl in the second ad; that he also told of correcting the condition of a man suffering from a skin ailment who had vainly visited a number of doctors and spent a lot of money — this after "several sessions"; that he told of "relieving" a boy who had come to him after having been

confined for mental treatment and who, under hypnosis, he
had discovered hated his mother; and finally how Masters
told his audience he had successfully used hypnosis to cure
"ulcers, alcoholics and narcotic addicts."

The state's witness Libby then testified that several days
later he returned and had a private interview with Masters
during which, under questioning, he related his imaginary ailments: that he had blinding headaches, nausea, pressure behind the eyeballs, extreme weakness, and dizziness. He told
how Masters questioned him closely about his health problems and marital status, and how he guilefully told Masters
that treatment by several medical doctors had given him no
relief.

The witness went on to relate that Masters told him he
thought he could help him by "hypnotherapy," and requested
$100 down in advance of treatment; how he told Masters he
didn't have that much money, but that he returned a few days
later and Masters accepted his check for $50 (which had later
been cashed by Masters and was introduced in evidence). He
then told how Masters thereupon lifted and carried him into a
rear office, placed him in a chair, questioned him further about
his family and medical background, and then told him to re-
lax, that his eyeballs were being drawn upward, that he was
growing sleepy, ever so sleepy, was sinking into a trance . . .

He told how Masters then bade him raise his right hand to
his forehead, which he did, and that Masters presently told
him that his trouble grew out of his hate for his father and
that he should banish this hate and think only kindly
thoughts; and then how Masters counted to four or five and
told him, Libby, that he was awake and would henceforth
have only blessed thoughts and would "think nothing but love
and kindness toward the entire world" — and instructed him
to make a future appointment. Finally Libby told how he had
faked his symptoms of being under hypnosis, all the time
being fully conscious of what was going on around him.

Another state's witness, a Dr. Klanke, a medical doctor of

twenty-five years' experience, testified that for fifteen years he had been using hypnosis as a means of curing certain physical and mental disorders; that in order to prepare for this he had, following his regular medical education, studied this specialized therapy at Cornell, the University of London, and UCLA, besides attending seminars. He testified that he never used hypnosis until he had made a complete physical examination of the patient and then only if he considered such a course an "absolute necessity." He said it was not safe for anyone to use hypnotherapy without a background of medicine because by its improper use a patient might be made worse off, even resorting to suicide.

Roy Masters chose not to take the stand, as was his right, but called on his behalf an expert witness, a specialist in chemical psychology, who guardedly testified that "there are people who use hypnosis who work with doctors" and that he knew of psychologists — inferentially not medical doctors — who sometimes used hypnosis as a method of treatment.

The testimony in, Roy Masters was convicted and was sentenced to serve thirty days in jail *and* pay a fine of $500. He appealed to the Texas supreme court, where he contended, among other things, that the trial court's jury instructions were bad; that Libby was an accomplice in any crime that was committed, and so should not have been allowed to testify; and finally that the evidence failed sufficiently to show that Masters had ever charged for his services.

Justice Morrison in his opinion batted down these objections in swift order: "It is clear from the record in this case that appellant [Masters] offered to treat a physical or mental disorder by a system or method and to effect a cure therefor, and that he charged money . . . and so we hold the evidence to be sufficient to support the conviction. . . . an undercover agent is not an accomplice witness so long as he does not bring about the crime, but merely obtains evidence against those engaged in the traffic. . . . This [the canceled check endorsed by 'Roy Masters Institute of Hypnosis'] we

hold to be sufficient evidence that appellant received money
for his services. . . . Affirmed."

It will be observed that no claim was made in the foregoing
case that the art or science of hypnosis is a fake, or that it
cannot be helpful in medical therapy, but only that Roy Masters was unlawfully practicing medicine by use of it and, as
suggested by Dr. Klanke, that the therapy ought to be used
only after thorough medical examination and administered by
an experienced medical doctor — an opinion upon which
there seems to be some divergence of views.

In the *American Law Reports* there is a fascinating annotation on "hypnotism as an illegal practice of medicine"
which opens thus:

"Experimentation with hypnotism and its uses in various
fields of medicine, such as an analytical aid in psychiatry or
as an anesthetic in obstetrics, has become increasingly prevalent in recent years. Often relegated to the position of being fit
subject matter for vaudeville performance, mysticism, or even
'black magic,' hypnotism is now more frequently recognized
as an effective scientific tool."

In support of this statement the annotation cites and
quotes briefly from a recent California case (1959) where the
resourceful attorney for the accused in a murder case asked
for and was refused by the trial court the right to have his
client examined in jail prior to his trial by an experienced
hypnotist in order to attempt a recall of his memory at the
time of the alleged murder. I dug out the case and read it.

It arose in a rather unusual way. A San Diego lawyer
called Harold Cornell was asked to come to the county jail to
see a man called Conrey, who was being held without bail on
a charge of first-degree murder. He went and talked to his
man, who told him he could remember nothing about his
movements or whereabouts the night of the homicide. Since
lack of memory is not ordinarily a defense to crime, or very
helpful to one's lawyer, the troubled counsellor went away
and did a little sleuthing on his own.

He discovered that on the fatal night his client had apparently been wandering from bar to bar in either a profound state of intoxication or shock, or possibly both. This still did not help very much. Then he remembered a professional hypnotist who had previously had success with stimulating memory recall by hypnosis. They conferred and the lawyer went to the sheriff and asked him to allow the hypnotist to see and examine his client.

"Nawthin' doin'," the sheriff in effect replied.

He then petitioned the county court where the trial would take place to compel the sheriff to let the hypnotist see his client but (more genteelly, one hopes) His Honor also turned him down. He then turned to the state supreme court, petitioning it for a writ of mandamus to compel the trial court to compel the sheriff to let the hypnotist have at his client.

His petition covered the facts just related, and was accompanied by a statement from the proposed hypnotist, Mikesell, in which he averred that for fourteen years he had been a practicing demonstrator and teacher of the art of hypnotism; that he had had considerable success with hypnotic "recession recall wherein the subject is unable to recall memories by reason of shock, amnesia, intoxication or the passage of time by voluntary recall and that under hypnotic influence recall . . . is induced and the subject is able to recall in detail incidents and activities which he was unable to recall voluntarily" and that he was of the opinion that the defendant Conrey might respond under hypnosis.

The respondent in resisting the mandamus argued that such an examination was a vain thing anyway and should be denied because the results would not be admissible in any event (he cited numerous cases involving the inadmissibility of statements obtained by hypnosis, truth serum, and lie-detector tests).

Justice Peters, speaking for the court, met this argument bluntly: "These cases have no applicability to the problem . . . They all deal with the admissibility of evidence . . .

[which] is not the question here presented. Cornell [the lawyer] is now seeking to learn facts that may be of assistance in preparing the defense. . . . He wants to ascertain, if possible, the accused's whereabouts on the night in question. . . . [Such] evidence so secured, whether or not . . . admissible, may put Cornell in possession of facts which, when followed up, would result in the discovery of admissible evidence that might constitute a complete defense. . . ."

Next, His Honor spoke of the constitutional right of an accused person to consult with counsel before trial in order to prepare a proper defense. "If an attorney is not given a reasonable opportunity to ascertain the facts [this right] . . . would be denied. . . . [It] is not limited simply to meetings between the client and his counsel. If necessary third persons may accompany counsel [such as an] . . . interpreter [or] psychiatrist. . . ."

The judge now came to grips with hypnotism itself.

"The use of hypnotism for the purpose desired is recognized by medical authorities. . . . There is no substantial legal difference between the right to use a hypnotist in an attempt to probe into the client's subconscious recollection, and the use of a psychiatrist to determine sanity."

His Honor now reared back and shifted into high:

"It is ordered that the writ of mandamus issue requiring the trial court to issue an order to the sheriff permitting the petitioner to examine the accused with the aid of a hypnotist. The order shall further provide that such examination be conducted in private unless the accused waives that right."

Returning again to the question of whether the practice of hypnotism constitutes an illegal practice of medicine, guilt or innocence often depends upon the precise wording of the particular state statutes defining the practice of medicine, which sometimes sharply differ. At least two states, Maine and Massachusetts, have presumably become Meccas for the harried hypnotists of America; each has a statute exempting hypnotists from having to be licensed or registered medical doctors.

And in an old Delaware case a lay hypnotist was held entitled to a jury instruction that he would not be guilty of illegally practicing medicine if he did not prescribe remedies or perform surgery for the cure of bodily disease or ailments.

But in a late California case (1961) under a statute similar to the one in the *Masters* case, which began this hypnotic essay, the lay hypnotist's conviction for illegal practice of medicine was affirmed, the court adding that while hypnotism might one day be recognized sufficiently to be licensed on its own, the legislature had not yet done so, and meanwhile medically unlicensed practitioners practiced at their peril. (This is not really in conflict with the California murder case just mentioned, for there the issue was not illegally practicing medicine by hypnotism but whether the accused should have been allowed to consult a qualified hypnotist under circumstances there outlined, and did not involve the practice of medicine.)

So there it is, and I never did learn who won that handsome bedroom suite. Anyway, hypnotism seems to have come a long way since the days I stood before Gately's window. And I haven't even touched upon the wide use of hypnotism in the heady world of spiritualism and faith healing.

ADDENDUM: Being curious to learn what happened later, I wrote Conrey's lawyer, Harold Cornell, who graciously wrote me that the murder charge grew out of the violent death of a woman his client had met during the fatal evening in a bar; that Conrey suffered from alcoholic amnesia; that he responded to hypnosis and was examined in the lawyer's presence by a hypnotist in five sessions lasting about two hours each; that he was examined with "pendulum response, automatic writing, and oral answers; that he put himself with the victim giving all details from 11:00 P.M. to 1:30 A.M. at the death scene except the killing. He broke on questions about the murder act [itself], but it was clear that he dragged the semi-nude . . . [woman] . . . to a slight depression near the graveyard and ran his car over her several times." Conrey was convicted of second-degree murder and sentenced to prison. Hypnotism was not mentioned during the trial. Speaking generally, Mr. Cornell also added: "By hypnotic recall we [once] traced an amnesia victim's wanderings for three months without missing a stop."

So the lawyer's guess was right; hypnotism had indeed made his client remember things he had forgotten. But regrettably for his case, that recall did not furnish him with a legal defense to the charge. Yet it might have, and Brother Cornell had made the good fight to find out.

Being a persistent cuss, I again wrote Mr. Cornell, asking if he would explain in more detail about the working of pendulum response and automatic writing, and again he kindly wrote me as follows:

"The pendulum response is a simple device for subliminal disassociation dependent upon unconscious manual reflex. It is usual to use a moonstone on the end of a fine jeweler's chain, but a large button on the end of a string or thread will do as well. The pendulum is held by the subject and dangles between the thumb and forefinger. First the response is conditioned by asking a series of obvious 'yes answer' questions with the subject nodding his head and observing the direction of the pendulum swing. The yes response is usually a forward and back swing. The same is done with 'no answer' questions; then his view of the pendulum is obstructed and questions asked and swing noted, with instructions to the subject to make no conscious movement of the pendulum. It works best with personal highly emotional questions and may exhibit a major conflict between conscious belief and subconscious disposition. You might find it interesting to try it on yourself as most of us have uncertainties from conflicts which we don't know exist.

"Automatic writing is accomplished by giving the subject pencil and paper with his vision of it obstructed. Let him doodle for a short time and then start questioning. This will not work against any subject resistance but usually the writing is legible in fairly well-spaced lines and appears almost normal except for disjointed continuity and interspersed illustrations. Under hypnosis the handwriting may change and childish handwriting will answer questions about childhood. Comparisons have shown this occasionally to be done in the handwriting of the subject at the age about which he is questioned."

I may add that from our correspondence Mr. Cornell emerges not only as an astute and resourceful lawyer, but a mighty interesting individual whose colorful background includes working as a stevedore, soldier, cowboy, truck driver, diesel engineer, wrestler, and teacher in such diverse fields as zoology, chemistry, physics, and the law. Who said lawyers must be dull and stuffy types?

7

Little Elmer

O N a fine August day some years ago, after his hay was in, a thrifty and prosperous upstate New York farmer by the name of Frank Palmer drove to town to visit his lawyer. The world had treated him kindly and he was in good health, but time was passing and he wasn't getting any younger and he wanted to draw his will. Besides his thriving farm, Farmer Palmer had acquired considerable livestock and other personal property. He was a widower; two of his daughters were grown and married; in addition to the hired help, with him on the farm lived two people: his favorite grandson Elmer Palmer, whose father was dead, and Elmer's widowed mother, Susan Palmer.

Farmer Palmer carefully explained his situation to his lawyer. He pointed out that his two daughters were married and comfortably off and so would not need much from him; and that, aside from seeing that his deceased son's widow Susan should continue to have a roof over her head if anything happened to him, he wanted his farm and all his property to go ultimately to his little grandson Elmer, the apple of his eye. Could this be done?

It could be done, Farmer Palmer's lawyer gravely assured him; and in due course Farmer Palmer left the lawyer's office, complacently patting the newly signed will in the breast pocket of his uncomfortable "town" clothes. In this document he left two small token legacies to his two married daughters, duly provided for the roof over the head of daughter-in-law Susan, and left the farm and the remainder of his considerable residuary estate to his little grandson Elmer, lock, stock, and barrel.

When he got home from town and gratefully out of his constricting blue serge suit, Farmer Palmer made his first grave mistake, and one that, in the light of developments, probably cost him his life. He took his fourteen-year-old grandson Elmer aside and proudly told him what he had just done. Now the law report from which this story is reconstructed unfortunately does not give us any extended description of little Elmer. But it is evident that he was quite a lad: imaginative, calculating, and relentlessly acquisitive. It also appears that little Elmer's main reaction upon learning of his grandfather's bounty was not one of gratitude for all that the old man proposed to do for him, but rather concern over how quickly grandpa might die so that little Elmer would the sooner take over the farm. Elmer was something of a juvenile monster, you see, a character straight out of Charles Addams.

Farmer Palmer's innocent blunder in telling his grandson of the provisions of his will still might not have cost him his life had he not, once this information was divulged, again got his blue serge suit out of mothballs and begun courting the Widow Bresee. But then again, perhaps dying for love is at least more romantic than merely dying. In any case, not only did Farmer Palmer woo the Widow Bresee, but in the spring, just about a year and a half after the will was drawn, he married her and, not unnaturally, took her home with him to live. Romance, however, had not prevented Farmer Palmer from first craftily entering into an antenuptial contract with the Widow Bresee in which she agreed not to claim any widow's dower rights in his property in the event of his death. The heady vapors of autumnal love had not clouded his canny judgment that much. This shrewd foresight was also quite a break for Elmer because otherwise the old man's will, leaving everything to Elmer, would automatically have been revoked by his marriage. That is the law. And little Elmer seems to have clearly understood all this. Now nearly sixteen, he still remained the apple of his grandpa's eye; despite the abundant allures of the Widow Bresee, Farmer Palmer still wanted little Elmer to have his fine farm and the bulk of his estate when he died. There was only one canker in all this for Elmer: the gnawing chance that dear old grandpa might change his mind about his will. What to do, what to do?

Again it is difficult to reconstruct from the bare legal report the morbid and steamy atmosphere that must have prevailed on the Palmer farm after the Widow Bresee came there to live. "Desire Under the Silo," it might be called. It is even more difficult to imagine that a sixteen-year-old farm boy could have thought of, much less understood, the fairly complex legal implications of the situation. The reported case unfortunately glosses over this tense human drama — but then the reading of law reports is frequently an exercise in austerity, not to say outright frustration. Judges seem to pride themselves so much on their lofty detachment from the realities of human emotion that one is occasionally tempted to shake them.

In any case it is clear from the reported case that at some time during the summer after his remarriage Farmer Palmer made his final and fatal blunder: he remarked in the hearing of his grandson Elmer that he was thinking of revoking his old will and making a new one. This sealed his doom. Acquisitive little Elmer now grew frantic; his worst fears were about to be realized. How could he keep from losing the precious farm? One can see him tossing and scheming at night in his bare farm bedroom. Then one night the answer came. Why hadn't he thought of it before? It was all so obvious. Just suppose that grandpa should suddenly up and die — just happened to, of course. Then he *couldn't* tinker with his

darned old will, could he? Or draw any new one? Little Elmer
was a youth of action; at dawn he arose and quick got hold of
some weed poison. That, alas, was the end of Farmer Palmer.

Unfortunately for little Elmer, some suspicions were
aroused over the abrupt agony of Farmer Palmer's departure.
An investigation was made — and little Elmer was charged
with murder. After a long and dramatic trial during which
Elmer unblinkingly maintained his innocence, he was convicted of second-degree murder and sentenced for a term of
years to the state reformatory. His extreme youth probably
saved him from a much heavier sentence than he got.

Now it might be supposed that this turn of events would
have dampened the spirits of little Elmer, that contrition
might have set in and that he might now have been satisfied to
serve his time and disappear into a grateful fog of obscurity.
But not Elmer; he was made of sterner stuff, and contrition
was not in him. Even in prison he still schemed to lay his hot
little hands on the farm and the rest of the swag for which he
had killed his own grandfather. So much did he covet it that
when his two aunts — the two married daughters of Farmer
Palmer — started a chancery suit to cut off Elmer under the
original will, Elmer hired himself not one but two lawyers
and squared away to fight the case.

A long hearing on the issue was held in the trial court.
Little Elmer was still in prison but in his absence his two
resourceful lawyers got in there and valiantly pitched for him.
The aunts, through their attorney, maintained that it was neither just nor equitable that Elmer should get his grandfather's
estate; that all the world knew he had murdered his grandfather to get immediate possession of the property for himself
and to prevent a revocation of the will. Such things simply
could not be. Elmer's resourceful lawyers boldly countered
that it made no difference whether Elmer had murdered his
grandfather. They correctly pointed out that there was no law
or statute in New York or anywhere else that prevented a
beneficiary under a will who had intentionally plotted the

death of his testator from still taking under the will; that Elmer was already serving his rap and that to rule against him would be to impose more punishment than the law specified; and that in any case the statutes on the subject of wills clearly provided certain unmistakable legal ways in which wills might be revoked — and murder was not one of them. "Follow the statute" was their argument in a nutshell, and it proved to be a powerful one.

When the dust of legal combat had settled the never-say-die Elmer had won his case; the fatally coveted farm was now close to his avid grasp. But the fatherless aunts were by this time thoroughly aroused; they appealed the decision to the Court of Appeals, the highest court in the state. The arguments there were even longer and more bitter than before. Then one day Judge Earl was ready to deliver the opinion of the court. By this time seven years had passed since the fateful will was drawn. Speed has never been a strong point of the creaking machinery of the law and little Elmer had served his time and was now free, pale, and twenty-three. We can only imagine his whirling thoughts as Judge Earl began delivering the opinion of the appellate court. At long last, *this* was it; the old farm was almost in his clutches. . . .

"At the date of the will, and subsequently to the death of the testator, Elmer lived with his grandfather as a member of his family, and at his death was sixteen years old," Judge Earl began. "He knew of the provisions made in his favor in the will, and, that he might prevent his grandfather from revoking such provisions, which he had manifested some intention to do, and to obtain the speedy enjoyment and immediate possession of his property, he willfully murdered him by poisoning him. He now claims the property, and the sole question for our determination is, can he have it?"

No record is left of Elmer's reaction to this ominous opening blast. Judge Earl continued with his opinion: "The defendant says that the testator is dead; that his will was made in due form and has been admitted to probate, and that, therefore, it must have effect according to the letter of the law."

Judge Earl then agreed that if the statutes pertaining to wills must be followed to the letter, as Elmer's lawyers maintained, and as the trial court had already held, this would indeed give property to the murderer of one who makes a will. We may guess that Elmer's spirits must have here risen a notch. "It was the intention of the lawmakers," the judge continued quietly, "that the donees in a will should have the property given to them." The judge doubtless paused here. One can almost hear him clear his throat. "But it never could have been their intention that a donee who murdered the testator to make the will operative should have any benefit under it. If such a case had been present to their minds, and it had been supposed necessary to make some provision of law to meet it, it cannot be doubted that they would have provided for it."

The good judge then proceeded to review the various ancient maxims of the law, including one of the oldest: "No man shall profit by his own wrong." He quoted Blackstone; he quoted Coke; he drew upon the Code Napoleon; he even quoted Aristotle in Latin. One suspects that had Aristotle been a Roman he would have quoted him in Greek. But the erudite judge was in a bit of a fix. For the plain truth of the matter was that the floundering Judge Earl had very little exact precedent to go on. This strange case was a new kettle of fish. Yet it is clear from his opinion that the judge was revolted to his gizzard by the notion that a murderer could inherit under the will of the man he had murdered; he was struggling to deny him if he could, even if he had to quote from the old cookbook.

He referred next to the earliest doctors, the blood-letting barbers. "There was a statute in Bologna that whoever drew blood in the streets should be severely punished, and yet it was held not to apply to the case of a barber who opened a vein in the street," he said. In his extremity he even poetically invoked God. "It is commanded in the Decalogue that no work shall be done upon the Sabbath, and yet giving the command a rational interpretation founded upon its design the Infallible Judge held that it did not prohibit works of necessity, charity or benevolence on that day."

Then he got down to cases. It was growing plain that he did not *like* little Elmer. "Here there was no certainty that this murderer would survive the testator, or that the testator would not change his will, and there was no certainty that he would get this property if nature was allowed to take its course. He therefore murdered the testator expressly to vest himself with an estate. Under such circumstances, what law, human or divine, will allow him to take the estate and enjoy the fruits of his crime?"

One can almost see the righteous old judge pause and glare down over his glasses at tense little Elmer. "The will spoke and became operative at the death of the testator," he went on inexorably. "He caused that death, and thus by his crime made it speak and have operation. Shall it speak and operate in his favor? If he had met the testator and taken his property by force, he would have had no title to it. Shall he acquire title by murdering him? If he had gone to the testator's house and by force compelled him, or by fraud or undue influence had induced him to will him his property, the law would not allow him to hold it. But can he give effect and operation to a will by murder and yet take the property? To answer these questions in the affirmative it seems to me would be a reproach to the jurisprudence of our State and an offense against public policy."

One can imagine that it had grown very quiet in the courtroom as the stern old judge pressed on to his conclusion. He now paused to blast the principle of an old North Carolina case cited by Elmer's lawyers, a case where a wife who had connived with her lover to murder her husband was nevertheless held entitled to her dower interest. One can almost hear him snort. "I am unwilling to assent to the doctrine of that case. . . . The widow should not, for the purpose of acquiring property, be permitted to allege a widowhood which she has wickedly and intentionally created." One again sees him pause to glare finally down at pale little Elmer. "The judgment in this case is reversed," he concluded.

The bailiff's hammer would now fall three times; it had the finality of doom. Judge Earl and his colleagues would gather up their rustling black robes and sweep austerely from the tall chamber; a heavy mahogany door would breathe shut. Little Elmer had at last got his comeuppance.

In reaching his decision old Judge Earl may perhaps be forgiven his indignant floundering and occasional flights of voluptuous rhetoric. It was a tough case. After all, when this bomb was dropped in his lap there was little legal precedent on the subject either in New York or elsewhere. You see, Farmer Palmer had made his will in 1880; little Elmer had dispatched him in 1882; and the final court decision itself was handed down 'way back in 1889 — many, many years ago. Little Elmer himself would now be a very old man if in fact he has survived all his disappointments and frustrations.

Since then the celebrated New York case of *Riggs v. Palmer* has become a landmark authority on this macabre subject in Anglo-American jurisprudence. A "leading case," as lawyers call it. Rarely does a similar new case come up in which it is not at least cited if not followed. And mostly it is followed. So the blood-letting barber from Bologna lives on and on. Thus did Elmer's talkative grandpa gain a lasting if dubious sort of posthumous fame. Most of us would doubtless prefer to take our little blaze of glory on a quiz program.

This old New York case is a beautiful example of judge-made law — or "judicial legislation," as its harsher critics might put it. The case also probably raised far more complex legal questions than ever it solved. Suppose the testator-killer is acquitted on his later criminal trial? Or the murder is not discovered until after distribution is made to the killer under the will? Or the killer is found insane? And what about those characters who kill their *intestate* or will-less relatives the more rapidly to take under the general laws of descent? Or to *prevent* the making of a will? Or what about life insurance beneficiaries who kill the assured to accelerate the death provisions under a policy? Or to prevent any change in beneficiaries? These are but a few of the macabre possibilities. Can the ancient maxim that the killer cannot profit by his wrong be made to fit all these diverse cases? If so, by what rule of logic or of law? It gives one a mild case of the judicial "bends" just to think of it. This is not to criticize the doctrine of the Riggs case; rather it is to suggest the possible ramifications of its doctrine — that and the capacity of the law to meet and grapple with new situations.

It would be moderately comforting to report that there have been only a few such cases since Grandpa Palmer got his for talking too much. Comforting, yes, but quite erroneous; the dusty lawbooks fairly abound with them. In fact, of late years the murdering of testators the quicker to get their property has reached mildly epidemic proportions. Alas, it seems that those traits of mankind which we call cupidity and greed have not subsided notably since 1882, nor apparently do murderously inclined testamentary beneficiaries, as a class, trouble too much to learn the law before they do their benefactors in. So this grisly seminar will not have been entirely wasted if it dissuades even one itching prospective devisee or legatee from dispatching his maiden aunt in vain. The moral of all this? Don't kill the talkative goose that made the golden will.

8

Rudolph the Red-faced Reporter

ALL of us have laughed and laughed at the misprints and goofs we occasionally run across in newspapers: "In his sermon yesterday Reverend Allen spoke eloquently of the three stages of man — childhood, adolescence and adultery" — and occasionally best-selling books have been pasted together out of the more amusing ones. But not all these typos have been quite so hilarious to the people immediately involved: to the reporter, to his paper, or to aggrieved readers claiming to be libeled by them. In truth some of the bitterest and most expensive litigation in the books has grown out of these innocently careless and "amusing" newspaper errors. Take the case of Minnie Hatfield of Hutchinson, Kansas.

Minnie Hatfield, spinster, inveterate churchgoer, lifelong doer of good works, returned from church one Sunday morning and composed herself in her rocking chair to read the Sunday morning edition of the Hutchinson *Gazette*. A titillating headline over a brief news item on the front page caught her eye: "RAIDED ROOMING HOUSE" — and palpitantly she read on. "Sheriff Scott Sprout yesterday raided the rooming house on First Avenue West, conducted by Ruth Newman. Two girls, Bess Stolen and Minnie Hatfield, were charged with being inmates of an immoral house, and the Newman woman with running one. They were released on $500 bail."

Minnie Hatfield stopped rocking and intently read the article again. There was no mistake, it said *Minnie Hatfield!* She sat rocking thoughtfully. She had lived in Hutchinson all her life and knew that her family were the only Hatfields in town and she the only Minnie. Who had perpetrated this cruel joke and why? Presently she folded the newspaper and, with pursed lips, marched grimly down the street to see Lawyer Williams. Sabbath or no Sabbath, there was work to be done.

Next day a stern Mr. Williams called at the editorial offices of the *Gazette* with the offending article. (One can see him smacking the newspaper with the back of his hand as he vented his indignation.) What is the meaning of all this? Who did this monstrous thing to a virtuous, innocent woman? And *why,* in heaven's name? One has to imagine the horrified scurryings that went on before it was discovered that a young reporter, a new man in town, was the villain of the piece; that he had seen Sheriff Sprout shortly before the Newman place was tipped over and been given the names of the "girls" but had regrettably mistaken the name of one of the real inmates, Minnie Olson, for poor dear Minnie Hatfield. We're so terribly sorry. What can we do? We'll correct it tomorrow and also run an apology.

Lawyer William promised nothing and went away. The next day the *Gazette* ran the same article again, correcting the offending name to Minnie Olson, but there was no further explanation and no apology. Minnie Hatfield was in no mood for equivocation; she again sped to see Lawyer Williams and in a few days the Gazette Printing Company was served with papers suing it for a small fortune in an action for libel.

In her declaration Minnie Hatfield set forth at length her grievances in lawyers' legalese: first, Minnie and her background; then the offending article; that it was untrue that she was now or ever had been the inmate of a bawdy house; and finally that the article had caused her "great mental anguish,

humiliation and grievous injury" to the tune of the large
amount of money she claimed. The scared *Gazette,* which
meanwhile had retained Smith & Smith, flatly denied everything; said the article did not refer to the aggrieved plaintiff
but to a prostitute; that moreover the whole thing was an innocent mistake that had been corrected; that in any case Minnie Hatfield had not been injured because her friends and
neighbors would be the first to know that the woman referred
to could not possibly have been she. Thus one day a jury was
chosen and the litigants squared away for their courtroom
battle.

Genteel Minnie appeared and with downcast eyes told her
simple story, including the fact that she was the only Minnie
Hatfield in town and had never even seen the inside of "one
of those dreadful places!" Next, certain of her friends and
neighbors appeared on her behalf and testified to the same
general effect and that they had known Minnie for years and
that it was violently untrue that she had ever been anything
but a woman of extensive good works and unblemished virtue. "Why, the very idea!"

The newspaper then had its turn and, through the har-
assed young reporter — who presumably had to be kept on
and his malarial presence endured long enough for him to tell
his story — testified that the whole thing had been an innocent mistake; that he did not even know Minnie Hatfield and
had no remote intention of hurting her; that the baffling error
was just one of those darned old things.

The testimony in, Minnie, through her lawyer, asked the
trial judge to give a peremptory instruction to the jury, that is,
in effect to tell her twelve peers that since no disputed question of law or fact was involved, the jury should simply retire
and determine the amount of damages it would award poor
Minnie. At this juncture the senior Smith of the law firm of
Smith & Smith arose and discreetly pointed out to His Honor
that the state of Kansas had a statute that provided that,
when in any defamation case the defendant denied (as his

client had already denied) that the offending matter was spoken or published of the plaintiff, "the plaintiff must prove at the trial the facts showing that the defamatory matter was published or spoken of him"; in other words, he boldly implied, Minnie had not proven her case because she had failed to show that she was the whore lady referred to. One would love to have seen Minnie at this point! Accordingly, Lawyer Smith continued blandly, if any peremptory instructions were to be given at all, it should be to find for the defendant.

The poor trial judge found himself in a terrible dilemma. Not only had he never been confronted with such a novel case before, but neither had the supreme court of his state. What to do? Well, a perspiring jury was sitting there champing to be instructed, so the perplexed judge sighed and figuratively tossed a coin and made his best guess: he denied Minnie's motion for a peremptory instruction and submitted the case to the jury on an instruction pretty much along the lines suggested by Lawyer Smith. The jury took the hint and promptly found in favor of the defendant newspaper. Minnie immediately appealed to the Kansas supreme court where, in due course Chief Justice Johnston, after reviewing the facts, delivered the unanimous opinion of the court:

"The publication in plain terms specifically charged the plaintiff, a single woman of unquestioned character and reputation, with unchastity and immorality," His Honor began. "As the imputation was untrue, malice is inferred, and of itself constitutes a libel. . . . The only excuse is that a mistake was made. . . . This is not a valid excuse. The imputation was just as hurtful as if the writer had been acquainted with the plaintiff, and had intentionally applied the charge to her. . . . There is no excuse for a false charge of unchastity and immorality . . . and one who makes it . . . does so at his peril."

Plain words, true, but His Honor still had that picky old statute raised by Lawyer Smith to get around, and he moved

briskly to that chore: "The provisions [of the statute] apply
to cases where there is indefiniteness as to persons defamed.
. . . Here there is no indefiniteness. The reference to the
plaintiff by name was specific; plaintiff was the only Minnie
Hatfield in the city. . . . The judgment is reversed, and the
case remanded for trial as to the amount of damages to
which plaintiff is entitled." Gallant Minnie had defended her
honor and won her case. The report does not tell us whatever
became of Minnie Olson. . . .

While the *Hatfield* case is one of the earliest of its kind to
be found anywhere, it would be wrong to conclude that Chief
Justice Johnston's stern words so terrified newspaper reporters at large that they read and were impressed, and, impressed, went away never to err again. Most of them probably
never heard of the case, and the fact is that there are dozens
and scores of later cases in the books remarkably like it —
and this is not counting all the many more cases that were
settled by apology or money, or by a mollifying combination
of both, or if tried were not appealed — since in most states
it is only the appealed cases that "get in the books."

The prevalence of libel actions against newspapers probably lies not in any special malevolence on the part of news-
papermen but rather in the fact that because of their very
nature newspapers must be produced under great pressure
and written on the run, often by busy and preoccupied reporters who simply lack the time to check all their sources carefully. The "deadline" is probably the worst devil of the piece.
But all this is still no legal excuse for a goof of this kind, and
perhaps this is one reason for the popular picture of the cynical newspaperman, so harshly skeptical and hard-boiled.

But not all reporters are that way, and sometimes their gul-
libility is touching to behold. Take the case of a young reporter who once worked — briefly, to be sure — for the fa-
bled James Gordon Bennett the younger on an old New York

newspaper. Perhaps to get into the spirit of the thing and give it a proper headline, one might call it "Will the *Real* President Palmer Please Stand Up?"

A half-drunken old moocher had just been picked up for public begging when the young reporter arrived at the police court to do his daily stint. On being arraigned the old man had given his name as Palmer and a friendly policeman, thinking he recognized the derelict, tipped off the young reporter that there might be a good human interest story lurking beneath the old man's seedy exterior. The reporter talked privately to the old man and was himself promptly mooched for his pains. Disillusioned, he tried to pull away, but the old man persisted. Give him the price of a drink, he wheedled, and he would give the young reporter an exclusive and shattering human interest story to end all human interest stories. The reporter swallowed the bait.

Clutching his little scoop to his bosom, he raced back to his desk and, writing furiously, barely filed his big story in time for the early evening edition. In a burst of creativity he even wrote the headline.

"President and Pauper," it proclaimed in the eye-catching manner of its time. "Speculator Dissipates a Railroad Magnate's Fortune," it continued. "In a Police Court at Last. Policeman recognizes in his Prisoner a former Wealthy Employer."

Then, like any competent young reporter, in his lead paragraph he gave a glowing lump-in-the-throat account of how a pathetic old half-drunken "tramp" called Palmer — this was back in those dear dead days before tramps turned into excessively compliant dames — had been arrested that very day for begging. All very sad, so sad . . . This done, he soared off into the wild blue yonder:

"Edward E. Palmer [meaning his pet tramp] was for several years president of the DeKalb Avenue Railroad Company in Brooklyn," he wrote, "and at one time was the president of a bank in that city. He had a charming family, an elegant residence on DeKalb Avenue, and was possessed of considerable wealth. He speculated in cotton and lost everything, and then took to drink. . . . He is not doing anything and has no means, and when arrested was trying to raise a drink to brace up his shattered system."

Meanwhile, back in Brooklyn, the real Thomas (not Edward E.) Palmer, who had himself been president of the DeKalb Avenue Railroad for eight years, the only officer of the railroad by that name, sat reading this moving human interest story in the bosom of his family in his home on DeKalb Avenue, where he still lived. So deeply moved was he by what he read that he sued and won — and the proud and unpredictable James Gordon Bennett presumably personally fired his gullible young reporter. Or maybe made him an editor.

The case not only again shows that in this area — imputing crime or disgraceful behavior to the innocent — newspapers goof at their peril, but that even if it is done in all innocence (here the result of a sly old moocher's hard-luck story), that still is no defense. "False information from an unreliable source is no defense," is the way a judge might soberly put it. In passing, one wonders why the paper did not defend on the ground that the tip-off policeman *had* made a "reliable" identification — but apparently he hadn't — or whether indeed he was not himself in on playing this cruel joke on the young reporter.

The case also shows that a mere discrepancy in the name of the person libeled (here between Edward E. and Thomas) is likewise no defense if a substantial number of people believe that the article referred to the "real" former president of the DeKalb Avenue Railroad.

Libels, of course, may occur against persons in articles where no names are given at all. To take a simple example, if our local newspaper writes a cute no-names-mentioned article implying that the mayor of our town went on a four-alarm bender last night and was picked up for disorderly conduct in a waterfront bagnio, it had better be true or the newspaper is in bad trouble and one reporter is surely out of a job. Thus in the "tramp" case just mentioned, the real President Palmer would doubtless still have won even if his name had not been mentioned so long as the description otherwise fitted him and not anyone else. All of which is a nice roundabout lawyers' way of saying that a libel may occur by description as well as by name.

As was said in one early case: "It is not necessary for a plaintiff to satisfy every description given in the libel, as otherwise one might libel with impunity, by adding to a description which everybody would understand, one which did not appertain to the person [defamed]." In fact, where it is plain from the main thrust of a newspaper story that only the plaintiff was intended, many courts will so instruct the jury as a matter of law, regardless of minor discrepancies. This business of how the jury is instructed can be crucial in any case, but it seems especially so in defamation cases, as the great Annie Oakley herself once ruefully found out.

Shortly after the turn of the century the "real" Annie Oakley, she of Buffalo Bill fame, was shocked one day to read in a newspaper this lurid headline: "Annie Oakley Arrested. Famous Woman Rifle Shot Locked Up on Larceny Charge in Chicago."

Bracing herself, she read on. "Annie Oakley, daughter-in-law of Buffalo Bill," the article said, "and the most famous rifle shot in the world, was arrested in Chicago, Monday, under a Bridewell sentence, for stealing the trousers of a Negro in order to get money with which to buy cocaine. This is the woman for whose spectacular marksmanship King Edward himself once led the applause in the courtyard of Buckingham palace." Being guiltless of an addiction either to stealing men's trousers or to taking cocaine, she immediately consulted her lawyer, who swiftly filed suit.

At the subsequent trial the defending newspaper showed that a person professionally calling herself "Anny Oak Lay," who had in fact once herself been an expert rifle shot and had performed with a rival Cody's wild west show, run by her husband S. E. Cody (no relation to Buffalo Bill), and who upon her arrest called herself Elizabeth Cody, was the person actually arrested — a wrenching enough story in itself.

Nevertheless the real Annie Oakley won her case, and on appeal the affirming higher federal court said that the article would plainly have warranted the lower court to peremptorily instruct the jury as matter of law that the real Annie Oakley was the person intended.

Yet in a companion Virginia case based upon a reprint of the very same article in a Virginia newspaper, it was held that the real Annie Oakley had no ground for complaint where a Virginia jury found for the local newspaper defendant under a general instruction that they might find either way — which is neither the prevailing law on the subject nor very good law. Perhaps that's why Annie went into federal court with her other case.

In plowing through all these musty old libel cases some evidence is found that at one time our American courts were tempted to plump for accepting the innocence of the newspaper blunder as a defense to cases of libel by mistake — or at least were going to permit a favorable charge to the jury to that effect. Thus in an old Massachusetts case (1893), one of the earliest we have found, the offending article said that "H. P. Hanson" had been arrested, whereas in actual fact it was an "A. P. H. Hanson" who had been arrested. In a suit by H. P. Hanson, the trial judge, in a nonjury case, found as a fact that the libel was not published of and concerning the plaintiff, and on appeal the state supreme court split five to four to sustain the ruling — a real judicial cliff hanger.

Justice Holmes (this was before he moved up to his long career on the U. S. Supreme Court) dissented so eloquently in that case that it may not be excessive to say that almost single-handedly he shaped the law to its present form, namely, that even an innocent mistake is not a legal defense to a libel of this sort; that, as an English judge once phrased it, "the inquiry is not what did the defendant mean in his own breast, but what did the words mean" to an ordinary sensible reader who knew the plaintiff. As a New York court said in a fairly recent case, adopting the rationale of Holmes's deep analysis in his historic dissent, "Unless the true intent of the publisher . . . is to be gathered from the . . . article, rather than from what the writer subsequently says was in his mind, innocent parties may suffer without redress." All this may tend to explain why the newspapers of America have failed to nominate Oliver Wendell Holmes the Second as their patron saint.

The most that "innocence" can do for the luckless newspaper, it seems, is that its presence, where shown, might go to possible mitigation of damages with juries. But that's a chancy thing; jurors in defamation cases (except in Virginia) have not shown themselves excessively pro-publisher in this kind of case — at least so far as this researcher's investigations have gone. Quite the contrary, in fact.

Decisions in this rather narrow furrow of the broad field of the law of defamation — namely, newspaper libel by mistake — have declined sharply in recent years. This may perhaps be credited to three things: one, better initial reporting; two, more careful editing; and, three — and probably most important — the fact that, the prevailing law now being so plainly what it is, most of these cases are being settled by resigned newspapers (or their insurers) before they ever come to trial. "What's the use, Cholly?" But human nature also being what it is — and newspapers what they are — it is probably not too wild a long shot to predict that one of these fine days an innocent grandniece of spinster Minnie Hatfield (observe I did not say granddaughter) might be suing still another luckless newspaper for planting *her* in a *maison de joie*.

9

Barely Victorious

O N a warm sunny Saturday in late June several years ago, Marvin Weissenborn and Harold Carter and their wives were engaged in the great national pastime of seeking a little respite from a week of heat and toil. They were driving to spend the weekend at Sunshine Gardens, a commercially operated recreation camp in southern Michigan. Marvin was an inspector in an automobile factory and his wife kept house for their three children, who were accompanying them. Harold Carter was a machinist and his childless wife Ruth worked in a supermarket.

They had visited Sunshine Gardens before and liked the place and had gotten to know other of the camp's regular patrons. Sure enough, when they arrived, they caught a glimpse of good old Earl Hildabridle, a sixty-two-year-old bachelor automobile worker, disporting himself about the pool, enjoying the fresh air and sunshine. They hurried to unpack and join him and the others.

The Sunshine Gardens was a 140-acre tract, mostly wooded, located just beyond the outskirts of Battle Creek and was run by the married couple who had owned it for fourteen years. The place catered largely to working-class people who wanted a measure of privacy but lacked both the time and money to seek it in plushier and remoter places. The owners maintained strict regulations against rowdyism and drinking, and violators were requested to leave, the state police being called if they failed to go quietly. Thus the Gardens tended to attract the sober and industrious, mostly in family groups, and it had been several years now since the police had been called to eject anyone.

Business was good that weekend at the Sunshine Gardens, and when the latest arrivals joined the others around the pool they found not only Earl Hildabridle but a number of new faces — if that is precisely the word — including children ranging from toddlers to teen-agers. So the Carters and the Weissenborns and their children greeted old Earl and met the new visitors and settled down to enjoy a quiet weekend of rest and relaxation. The pastoral scene around the pool that lazy Saturday afternoon was doubtless one being duplicated in scores and hundreds of places throughout the country. There was only one slight difference: none of the people around *this* pool were wearing a stitch of clothing; all were as naked as the day they were born. The Sunshine Gardens was a nudist camp and every adult there was a dedicated believer in the practice of nudism.

Though the police had not been called to Sunshine Gardens for several summers, they occasionally dropped by to check on things, and they were on cordial terms with the proprietors. They had, in fact, last visited the place about two weeks before, finding several nudists enjoying themselves on that occasion, but there was no trouble and the police did not bother anyone. But on this particular Saturday afternoon, the weekend the Carters and Weissenborns chose to visit Sunshine Gardens, the police paid another surprise visit.

This time there were again two of them and this time their attitude was something less than cordial: they swiftly radioed for reinforcements — which arrived in speeding squad cars in a matter of minutes — and rounded up everyone on the place, including the Carters and Weissenborns and Earl Hildabridle, photographed them in the raw, questioned them, and finally booked some and released others. In the parlance of the police, after fourteen years of what might be termed uninhibited exposure, the Sunshine Gardens had been "tipped over" with a vengeance.

After assessing the evidence the police and prosecution decided to make an example out of the Carters and Weissenborns and also Earl Hildabridle. These five were formally arrested and charged with the crime of indecent exposure. Perhaps this course was pursued because these particular defendants were more or less regulars at the Sunshine Gardens; perhaps also because the state charitably did not want to involve too many children and neophyte nudists in the unsavory affair; perhaps too because these particular defendants had more vocally resented this unceremonious police intrusion into their privacy than had the others. Whatever the reason, formal charges were actively pressed only against these five: the two married couples and the bachelor Hildabridle, the others presumably being told to go clothe themselves and sin no more.

All five defendants pleaded not guilty upon their arraignment and their cases were consolidated for trial. The Michigan statute under which they were charged provides that "any person who shall knowingly make an open or indecent exposure of his or her person or the person of another" shall be guilty of a crime triable in circuit court. So it was there that they were tried and all five were swiftly convicted by a jury of laymen. The judge placed each defendant on two years' probation, imposing additional thirty-day jail terms as well as fines and costs aggregating $350 against each. They promptly appealed to the state supreme court.

There they urged among other things that there had been an illegal search and arrest on private property; that the "indecent exposure" statute was never intended to apply and did not apply to confirmed nudists who practiced their beliefs in private; that the statute is too vague and indefinite; and that in any case it is plainly directed at obscene exposures and that mere nudity is not in itself obscene nor is every exposure indecent, particularly where, as here, there was no evidence that the exposure offended the morals or sense of decency of those properly present and there were no overt acts of indecency or obscenity aside from the mere state of nudity itself.

Chief Justice Dethmers was assigned the case in the supreme court and he delivered himself in a terse three-and-a-half-page opinion — terse for a judge, that is — first reviewing the facts as he saw them:

"Two State police officers had gone on business to Sunshine Gardens, a nudist camp operated on private property in a secluded area," he began. "While there they had seen certain nude persons, secured their names and obtained warrants for their arrest. Thereafter, 1 of those 2 officers, in company with another officer, went to the camp with the warrants to arrest the persons therein named. While there, they saw other naked men, women, boys, and girls, out of doors, some standing, some sitting, some walking around, several in the vicinity of a pool, all exposed to the view of each other. Included were the defendants, adults, and also 4 girls then 8, 10, 11 and 12 years of age, respectively, and a 17-year-old boy, before whom the defendants stood nude with private parts exposed. The officers then and there arrested defendants. Their prosecutions ensued."

Then, waxing a little poetic and indignant, he had this to say about their briefs and arguments in favor of nudism:

"We decline to take the excursion into the field of the definitions, desirability, and delights of nudism, psychiatric considerations or purportedly applicable quotations from the Scriptures suggested in the briefs, or the flights of fantasy to which the subject may beckon. Consideration will be limited to questions of law raised by appellants, of which most are scarcely novel and none deserving of extended discussion."

He next addressed himself to their legal arguments:

"These points have been considered and answered in *Peo-*

ple v. Ring . . . and the cases therein discussed. . . . As indicated in *Ring* . . . the average jury, composed of members of the community, can be expected to represent and embrace a cross section of the community thinking and moral standards which are first reflected in the legislative enactment by the people's chosen representatives and, once again, in the statute's application to the facts of the case by the jury in arriving at its finding and verdict that certain conduct is violative thereof. That a jury found it to have been violated by defendants' exposure of their persons to the young children in this case and the exposure of the children themselves should be surprising to neither the pure in heart nor the lewd."

He then drew upon even loftier authority, referring to a recent U. S. Supreme Court "obscenity" case as follows:

"In *Roth v. United States,* . . . the court considered statutes couched in the same general terms as those of the statute before us, the words 'obscene' and 'indecent' having been employed there, as here, without further definition. The court held that the statutes, applied according to the proper standard for judging obscenity, do not violate constitutional requirements of due process by failing to provide reasonably ascertainable standards of guilt. The court further held that obscenity is not, as defendants here claim for nudism, within the area of constitutionally protected freedom of speech and, finally, that the proper standard for judging obscenity . . . is whether, to the average person, applying contemporary community standards, the conduct in question has a tendency to excite lustful thoughts. . . . Nakedness has not . . . been held an essential element of that right [freedom of assembly]. . . . The convictions should be affirmed."

In summary, then, Chief Justice Dethmers held that it was no ground for a successful appeal that the "indecent exposure" statute failed to define its terms or that it possibly invaded the constitutional rights of the defendants, it being sufficient that a jury of laymen found their deportment to be obscene and indecent.

The case had been argued and submitted at the April term of the supreme court and, in accordance with its practice, the affirming opinion of Chief Justice Dethmers was circulated privately among the other seven justices when it was written so that they might make up their minds whether to join in it or dissent. Among these others was Justice Voelker, then the second-newest man on the court and himself a former prosecuting attorney — a job which may be briefly defined as that of a district attorney without quite all the glamor.

Busy as he was, and beseiged by his own batch of assigned cases clamoring to be written, the case nevertheless bothered Justice Voelker. Could he in good conscience join in this opinion affirming the convictions of these nudists? He decided to dig deeper into the case to see what he could see. He plowed through all the voluminous testimony, not only at the circuit court trial but also at the preliminary examination. And the more he dug the more bothered he became. Finally he concluded he simply had to dissent and so he sighed and sat down and wrote out an opinion of his own.

Beginning gently, he suggested that more facts were needed, pointing out that the proofs showed that when the police arrived there was not the slightest evidence of obscenity or indecency. "Except for the fact that they were entirely unclothed," he wrote, "they might have been any group of people enjoying a rural weekend outing. As one of the officers testified at the trial, 'Well, some were standing, others walking around, some were sitting, children were playing on playground equipment.' " He showed that the defendants were working-class people nearing or past middle age, that all had previously visited the camp and were nudists by conviction, and that none had ever been convicted of any serious crime, sexual or otherwise. He then showed that the police, aside from removing upon request an occasional drunk or curiosity seeker — the last one three years before — had received no complaints about the place or its patrons during the entire period of its operation.

Warming to his task, Justice Voelker now let go with a small preliminary blast. "So the presumably outraged community boils itself down to a knot of determined police officers who, for some undisclosed reason, after 14 years made up their minds to set a trap and tip over the place. And tip it over they did."

He next showed that the earlier "business" visit on June fifteenth, alluded to by his Brother in his opinion, was but part of the rather obvious police strategy to get evidence on which to obtain warrants for the arrest of the three nudists they had then seen — one a woman — so that, thus armed, they would have some sort of legal excuse to return to serve them on June thirtieth — the day of the mass raid. "That the ostensible warrant-serving party of June 30th," he continued, "was in reality a planned new raid for bigger game — with the warrants for these three other persons serving as the legal foot-in-the-door — is shown by the fact that 3 carloads of cruising police officers joined the first car of warrant-serving officers within less than 2 minutes of a radio call. Now our experience with raids on nudist camps is mercifully limited, but we very much doubt that it would take 4 carloads of police officers to gather in the 3 nude defendants named in the June 15th warrants — and one of them a woman."

It was now growing plain that Justice Voelker meant to spring these defendants if he could. "That the officers may have been disappointed over the results of their earlier alleged 'business' visit and wanted to wait for a bigger week-end bag, including children (June 15th was a week day; June 30th fell on a Saturday), is of course sheer speculation," he continued, "but the fact is that the ultimate lack of warrants for the arrests of *these* defendants did not appear measurably to deter these same officers in making their mass arrests without warrants on June 30th."

Justice Voelker's next blast left no doubt where he stood: "It was indecent," he thundered in high dudgeon, "indeed the one big indecency in this case: descending upon these unsus-

pecting souls like storm troopers; herding them before click-
ing cameras like plucked chickens; hauling them away in police cars and questioning them over five hours; and then, final
irony, swearing out warrants that *one of their own number*
was the aggrieved victim of an indecent exposure."

Justice Voelker quickly reloaded his cannon and fired another salvo: "If these convictions can stand . . . then
henceforth police officers may raid at will locker rooms, art
classes, sunbathers at home and at picnics and beaches . . .
wherever they may decide by barracks room debate that a
suspected practice is immoral or indecent. . . . It would be
to impose not the moral standards of the community but the
moral standards of the patrolman on the most intimate and
private concerns of life."

Returning to hammer away at the "community standards"
theme, he quoted approvingly from the bristling dissent of
Justice Douglas in the *Roth* case already cited by his colleague, including the following: "Any test that turns on what
is offensive to community standards is too loose, too capri-
cious, too destructive of freedom of expression. . . . Under
that test, juries can censor, suppress and punish what they
don't like. . . . This is community censorship in one of its
worst forms [and is a] battle . . . the Philistines are certain
to win." Justice Voelker then added to this his own comment:
"We reject any test or rule that would make a juryman the
omniscient community litmus of that to which, by hypothesis,
neither he nor the community has ever been exposed. If
trained judges on this Court can disagree on the applicability
of this statute to these facts, we can see no merit and much
danger in a rule that can ignore and reject our differences in
favor of the presumably infallible intuitions of the average lay
juryman. . . ."

He then pounced gleefully upon some of the pearls he had
dredged up during his research: that the original complaints
and warrants had named one of the raiding police officers as
the victim of the exposure; that the informations filed in circuit

court had named nobody; and that his colleague's opinion
now seemed to plump for the children as the aggrieved ones.
He implied that for the police suddenly to claim shock over
nudism after patrolling the Sunshine Gardens for fourteen
years was akin to a waterfront prostitute crying rape the third
day after the fleet was in. This brought him down to the little
children, about which his Brother had dilated in his opinion.

"They were mercifully spared participation in the trial of
this case," he began, "but to surmise without a shred of evidence that they were corrupted by seeing their mother and
father without any clothes (along with some other mostly
middle-aged people some distance away) is gratuitously to
invest childhood with evil and erotic tendencies before mere
nakedness and to reject the observations and researches of
virtually every anthropologist and sociologist who has contributed to the literature of human mores." Here the judge
cited several authorities to back up his contention.

Plainly nettled and still bothered by his Brother's emotionally charged reference to the children, he pressed on: "Now
concern for little children is always touching and understand-
able, and my colleague possesses no exclusive franchise on it;
but if these convictions must be affirmed simply because my
associate thinks the prosecutions and the jury verdict may
have been inspired by a concern for children, we suggest that
there might have been other statutes and apter procedures
available to such an end. Moreover, and whether other
courses were available or not, the presence of children constituted no valid ground for . . . arresting these defendants for
an exposure which neither the proofs show, nor obviously
none of the participants regarded, as indecent."

Still he labored to remove the sting of the children, suggest-
ing that if their presence was now all that made this exposure
indecent, would it have ceased to be indecent had they been
absent and, if so, why. "To my mind the presence of the children, far from accentuating any indecency, was itself additional proof and insurance that no indecency or immorality

was contemplated or intended by these defendants," he asserted. "It is particularly monstrous to think that their parents would intentionally have exposed their children to that which they thought was indecent, and if they nevertheless had, which the people now seem to claim, then the prosecution should be censured for not taking far more drastic action to punish all concerned and to save the children from any repetition.

"So much for the presence of the children in this case."

Having bedded down the little children, Justice Voelker now turned the judicial searchlight on the statute itself, rather apologetically introducing his new excursion as follows:

"Lest I henceforth be heralded as the patron saint of nudism (which I probably will be anyway), I hasten to preface what follows by stating that I am not a disciple of the cult of nudism. Its presumed enchantments totally elude me. The prospect of displaying my unveiled person before others, or beholding others thus displayed, revolts and horrifies me. I think these people have carried an arguably valid basic idea (the deliberate de-emphasis of the prevailing Western body taboo, with the anticipated lessening and ultimate disappearance of the undoubted eroticism frequently attendant upon such taboo — that is, the very opposite of indecency) to excessive lengths.

"Having said all that, I have at once veered to the heart of this case. It is this: whatever I or my associates (or the circuit judge or the prosecutor or the police, for that matter) may personally think of the practice of nudism has nothing to do with the case. More controlling is the fact that there are a number of earnest people in this world (including these defendants) who do subscribe to organized nudism and who think that it is morally, mentally and physically healthful. But we need not speculate on or defend or attack the philosophy of nudism. The question before us is much simpler. Were these defendants guilty of making an indecent exposure? I say no."

He continued with tongue in cheek: "It is said that there are hardy bands of sincere and earnest folk among us who likewise insist that all mental, moral and physical health depends absolutely upon the regular consumption of vast quantities of bran. Others possess a similar passion for goats' milk. Few molest them or even bother their heads about them unless they too strenuously try to impose their beliefs upon those who happen to loathe these things. Thus, on the facts before us, do I equate the criminality of private social nudism — at least so far as a violation of this statute is concerned. Private fanaticism or even bad taste is not yet a ground for police interference. If eccentricity is a crime, then all of us are felons."

He pounded away at the implication that mere nudism was in itself obscene: "From the undoubtedly valid premise that some degree of nudity must always be involved in order for an exposure to be indecent, the *Ring Case* and the opinion of my Brother in this case have leapt to the erroneous conclusion that nudity is synonymous with indecency; the opinions imply that the more nudity present the more indecent the exposure. Both cases proceed upon the basic assumption that nudity in itself is obscene or indecent. As I shall presently undertake to show, this is a demonstrable fallacy. If this assumption were valid few artists could continue to work from live models, or, veering somewhat to a related field, the curators of our art galleries and museums would have to turn to the cultivation of fig leaves; and that stalwart badge of middle-class respectability, the *National Geographic* magazine, would be banished from the hearth to the censor's shears."

He now got down to cases, outlining nine hypothetical situations involving various forms of nudism, ranging from the high-stepping red-faced college drum major whose trousers split asunder before wildly cheering thousands during the Big Game, the sleepwalking inadvertent nudist, and on through the case of the lusting pathological exhibitionist, among others. In passing he implied that there was more real eroticism

displayed on any day on any public beach than this by these
sober middle-aged folks, however deluded, who occasionally
met away from the rush and din to crawl out of their work-a-
day clothes and sun themselves in the raw.

From his exploration and examples he conceded that an
exposure, to be indecent, need not also necessarily be public,
posing the case of the furtive exhibitionist who specializes in
female audiences of one (he might also have given that of
those culture-starved attendants at private stag parties devoted to staging animated tableaux depicting some of the
more exotic variations on the rites of love). He also conceded
that the exposees need not be confined to the pure and innocent (again the stag party might have served), but he equally
insisted that though conduct involving nudity might be both
immoral and unlawful, that did not also necessarily make it
"indecent," in the statutory sense. Thus, he implied, while
adulterous encounters are plainly immoral, unlawful, and
also universally grounds for divorce, they still do not become
"indecent" under the statute if the principals confine their cal-
isthenics to the bedroom — and surprise raids by armies of
policemen could not alter that fact. He was now ready to venture some generalities about what he deemed to be the true
meaning of the "indecent exposure" law. The most important
of these, he insisted, was the intention of the exposer.

Had these same nudists paraded down the main street of
Battle Creek in regimental garb, their exposure would doubtless be adjudged indecent, he declared, not so much because
most viewers would be shocked by the spectacle but rather
because, in the circumstances, it must have been the primary
intention of the nudists to inflict shock. Community standards, then, were important not as a rigid test of whether a
majority of the community might go and do likewise —
which allowed for no deviation in individual expression and
virtually guaranteed the guilt of the nonconformist — but
rather as those elusive standards might supply a clue to the
intention of the offender himself.

Finally, he likened the exposure by the nudists in this case to the imagined case of the police placing a ladder against a private home and watching a disrobed family disporting itself in the bathroom of a Saturday night, declaring that both must be held guiltless of indecent exposure because neither *intended* the exposure indecently. In a nutshell, he implied, snoopers can scarcely claim to be shocked by what they behold, and a raid by the police no more converts an innocent exposure into an indecent one than the absence of the police can convert an indecent exposure into an innocent one. The big subject of inquiry, then, in all indecent exposure cases is the frame of mind of the exposer: what did he intend? And since rarely if ever does even the most crude exposer declare his intention — "Look, lady, I'm being indecent" — that intention must usually be gathered from his actions judged in the light of *all the circumstances*. Thus judged, he insisted, the exposure of these nudists was not indecent. At the very least the issue was shrouded in doubt — a doubt which under our law had to be resolved in favor of the defendants.

Justice Voelker, evidently a bit of a card, now showed that he too could wax poetic and indignant: "Guilt or innocence of indecent exposure is not a matter of measuring the amount of human flesh exposed; one does not caliper the revealed epidermis and certify guilt as increasing by the square inch; the indecency of an exposure is always a matter of intent to be gathered from all of the circumstances," he declared. "The plain fact is that often the less the exposure the more plainly indecent it becomes, *by that very circumstance alone;* the plain fact is that usually there is involved an aggressive and unmistakably erotic attempt to focus the attention of others solely on the sexual organs of the exposer, and, as any weary patrolman knows (if some judges may have forgotten), most usually on a certain engorged portion of the male anatomy. To link these poor defendants, however deluded, with such gross and panting immorality is a kind of back-handed indecency in itself.

"Most simply put, then, where the exposure is neither meant nor taken as indecent there cannot be a violation of this statute. Unless this opinion were written entirely in vain, I should by now have demonstrated at the very least that a reasonable doubt exists that this statute applies to the conduct of these people. It is elementary under our Anglo-American legal system that where such a doubt exists the vote must be for innocence."

Heading now into the homestretch, Justice Voelker paused and gathered himself for a thunderous conclusion: "In a world locked in a death struggle between the David of democracy and the Goliath of giant totalitarianism, it serves David illy for the court of last resort of one of democracy's greatest industrial bastions — the State of Michigan — to put its stamp of approval on such a dubious departure from our traditional procedures and historic safeguards against invasion of our individual rights — the right to be secure from unreasonable search and seizure and the right in all criminal proceedings to receive the benefit of any reasonable doubt."

He even tried his hand at the satiric: "That these defendants may have been raided, arrested and prosecuted from the loftiest of motives is no answer; it is no excuse that the bold invasion of individual rights and liberties unfolded here was motivated by pureness of heart. These defendants can take little comfort that they are prosecuted with love and their conviction accompanied by a warm glow of community virtue. The busiest snoopers and moral vigilantes among us are doubtless convinced of 3 things: of their own unfaltering rectitude; that what they do is always for our own best good; and that any among us who dare question their activities are soaked in sin."

He closed on a lofty note: "For all practical purposes this is probably the court of last resort for these defendants; we are their last hope. Whatever we may privately think about the practice of nudism should not cloud our decision in this case. Our reversal of these convictions is no more an endorsement by us of nudism than our occasional necessary reversal of a murder conviction constitutes a judicial endorsement of murder. If nudism must go in Michigan it must go by right not might. The bald inescapable fact is that the prosecuting officials in this case badly overreached themselves. The time has now come for us to say so."

He then delivered his decision:

"The convictions are reversed and the defendants discharged. All film and prints of the defendants in the possession of the prosecution shall be returned forthwith to their counsel."

The final outcome? Four to three for reversal, with one justice abstaining. To coin a phrase, the nudists escaped by the skin of their teeth.

The foregoing case (*People v. Hildabridle*) is interesting not only on its own rather bizarre facts, but for its overtones. The case reveals far more than any mere expanse of sunburned skin. For one thing, it shows how sharply men of undoubted goodwill can differ over identical facts. For another, it shows that the law is often what men make it, and that even judges occasionally have hearts and emotions by which, contrary to popular mythology, they are sometimes ruled as much as by "The Law." It shows how wide is the gulf that can divide judges as well as other men, and that perhaps humility and compassion and a capacity for empathy figure in it somewhere. It shows that an important public issue — whether snoopers may claim to be shocked by what they behold — can be resolved by a soberingly narrow margin. Above all, the majority decision recognizes man's infinite capacity for folly and reaffirms the divine right of every man to be a damned fool in his own way so long as he does not too much bother others with his queer notions. It also shows that there are still earnest souls in high places who would question the exercise of that right by their nonconforming fellows. Finally, the case shows that the battle for tolerance is eternal.

The Dictionary and Jim Darneal

S OME fifty years ago bearded Old Man Garrison and his two daughters lived in a tent on the banks of a small creek in a remote area of Leflore County in the recently admitted state of Oklahoma. Old Garrison made a kind of chancy living by fishing, supplemented by the produce of an unkempt truck garden. The reported case is regettably sparse in its facts, but one gathers that the old man and his daughters lived pretty much to themselves, shunning their few neighbors, including the Darneal boys, who lived a few ridges away.

One night at dusk the tent of Old Man Garrison and his daughters was visited by a strange delegation — a troupe of angry shouting women. This horde of cackling females grabbed the old man, dragged him from his tent, beat and whipped him, and wound up by cutting off his hair. Then, shouting and laughing, the invaders ran off into the night.

When he was able to be up and around again Old Man Garrison sought out the sheriff and swore out a warrant, following which a group of young men in the neighborhood — not women — was arrested and charged with the crime of committing riot, contrary to an Oklahoma statute. This statute additionally provided that "if such person . . . at the time

of the riot . . . was disguised . . . he is punishable by im-
prisonment in the penitentiary not exceeding ten years and
not less than two." In other words, the legislature had or-
dained that ordinary rioting was bad enough but that rioting
while disguised was a felony.

At their trial in the county court all of the young men were
convicted of the felony of rioting while disguised and each
was sentenced to serve the minimum of two years. One of
them was young Jim Darneal, who asked for and had his case
severed and then appealed separately to the supreme court of
Oklahoma, urging among other things that whatever else he
might have been guilty of that night he was not *disguised*
within the meaning of the statute.

At his earlier trial in the county court the state's evidence
had disclosed that on the evening of the alleged riot Jim Darneal "was dressed almost entirely in the wearing apparel of a
woman, such as skirt, waist, and hat. His face was partly con-
cealed by clothes and rags wrapped around his head. *His
eyes, nose, mouth, and a portion of each cheek were exposed.*" (Emphasis added.)

At his trial the defendant had been identified by the victim
Garrison and his oldest daughter by his voice, their familiar-
ity with the feminine clothes he wore, and by his exposed
features. In other words, they recognized him. On his appeal
Jim Darneal argued that the fact that his alleged disguise was
so readily penetrable showed clearly that he was not "disguised" within the meaning of the statute and that accordingly the prosecution should fail and his conviction be reversed for insufficient evidence.

In the supreme court Mr. Justice Matson disposed of this
argument briefly, almost with laconic weariness, stating that
in essence it boiled down to the unacceptable proposition that
"there may be no conviction . . . unless the participants are
so completely disguised as to make it impossible to identify
them; that is, a prosecution will only lie under this statute
when it is impossible for the state to prove the offense. Such a

construction would render the statute a dead letter." After some further talk about the dictionary definition of "disguise" he affirmed the conviction and Jim Darneal went off to prison.

Before commenting on the result reached in this case, one cannot help wondering whether this old statute was not aimed mostly at such organized groups as the KKK. After all, the state was still less than thirty years from the first territorial land rush, even less far from its statehood, and the brave new legislature was probably trying its best to put down any lingering vestiges of the prevalent masked vigilantism of the roaring old territorial days.

If this was indeed the primary purpose of the act, I think it should have lent added force to Jim Darneal's argument because, one gathers, galloping vigilantes and other masked riders committed and still generally do commit their outrages while completely and uniformly disguised. One speculates also why these young men of the neighborhood so roughed up old Garrison in the first place. Was it a quarrel over fishing rights? Had the crusty old man forbidden the neighbor boys to court his daughters? Or had the whole thing started as a boyish prank that misfired? The tersely reported case gives not a clue.

The case does clearly show, however, how precarious freedom can be; how it can often depend upon how the dictionary defines a single word — "disguised" here — and moreover on how a judge in turn interprets that definition. The annotator of the source where I ran across this odd case agrees with Justice Matson. While I do not condone the cowardly behavior of Jim Darneal and his companions that night toward an old man, I find myself disagreeing with the decision. I think I might well have written to reverse. And I say this while only mentioning in passing the interesting related question of whether this was a riot at all — a point which was not even raised in the case. It seems clear that the young men were guilty of some form of assault, but they were not charged with that but rather with *rioting* while *disguised*. But rioting or no, I think a much graver question was whether young Darneal *was* disguised.

Justice Matson says in his opinion, as noted, that to follow the appellant's argument would render the "disguise" statute a dead letter. That does not necessarily follow. Fully disguised men, such as bandits and bank robbers, are caught and unmasked and imprisoned right along. Others are ultimately identified by fingerprints or by confederates or by recovered loot or by their voices or a limp or some other means.

Hard cases may make bad law, as Holmes said, but I think in this case I would have resolved the doubt in favor of not making a felon out of foolish young Jim Darneal. When a man's eyes, nose, mouth and cheeks — in other words, his face — are so exposed to his close neighbors that they can readily recognize him at dusk, and he is still held to be disguised, one wonders how he would go about getting himself *un*disguised. I further think that my dictionary bears me out and that His Honor either had a bad day or a poor dictionary or else he confused the state of being costumed with that of being disguised. They are not the same thing. By two years in prison they are not.

I feel another small digression coming on and, exercising my usual iron self-discipline, I shall yield to the impulse and succumb at once. From time to time in this book I have poked more or less amiable fun at some of the judicial opinions I have quoted from. Some of them are really pretty hard going and I now pause and explore the subject a little more.

Carry Nation, that intrepid soul who used to go around chopping down saloons — or was it up? — one day desisted long enough in her bar-hacking to do a pretty good hatchet job on judges. They were, she declared, nothing but a bunch of "nicotine-soaked, beer-besmeared, whiskey-bloated, red-nosed devils." (No one-track castigator she, she once called William McKinley "the brewers' President.") As a former judge I must loyally demur. After all, I never much cared for beer — either swallowed or smeared on — and I seem to recall that the noses of most of the hard-drinking judges I knew were rather more purple than red. But possibly this is the hairsplitting of a pedant.

Had the lady said instead that the average judicial opinion is among the dullest and murkiest reading in the world, and that the chances are bright that a judge's prose will be purpler than his nose, I would feel less inclined to dissent. Heaven knows that turgid and overblown writing is no novelty anywhere, alas, but why men trained in the law should so frequently be among the guilty has long puzzled me.

After all, the effective use of language lies at the heart of the law; its practitioners use it constantly in their briefs and opinions, in their wills, leases and other legal instruments, in their drafting and interpretation of our myriad statutes. The idea of superior rhetorical persuasiveness and suavity is crudely implicit in the popular expression describing the lawyer as "the great mouthpiece." Indeed, men of the law may be said to *live* by the word, its nuances, its fine distinctions, its subtle overtones. Why, then, are they so often inept at using it? I have some ideas that may partly explain the phenomenon. But only partly. The rest is mystery.

Lawyers possibly become so word-conscious during their long training and practice — and from repeated exposure to the dubious example of their predecessors — that by the time they get to the bench they are apt to have forgotten that glory of our language, the simple declarative sentence. From long immersion they come to feel that everything that is said or written must be hedged, hemmed, guarded, explained, restrained, refined, and larded with provisos, whereases, nevertheless, including-but-not-limited-to's, and all the rest of the mystic jargon of the law.

An additional compulsion to a rigid conformity of expression is that many of the law's pet words and phrases have been sanctified by judicial interpretation, so that any rebellious lawyer who dares indulge in the refreshing luxury of plain talk risks more than the reproving frowns of his brethren: he may lose his case along with his client. I suspect, then, that a good deal of our bad legal writing springs ironically not so much from a lack of concern with the word — the usual cause — but rather from an *over*concern with it. Hence it is that so many judicial opinions remain forever inscrutable to the layman.

For every Holmes or Cardozo, who at their best wrote a kind of luminous legal poetry, there are a thousand judges who appear to write with their feet, whose main discernible aim seems to be to impress and project a Socratic image rather than to illuminate, who contrive resolutely to grind out long, windy, repetitive opinions aswarm with clichés, platitudes, euphemisms, archaisms, stilted phrases, icy abstractions, ponderous latinisms, "inside" phrases, florid figures of speech and, worst of all, a pervasive aura of murk.

Whatever the reason, there is something about legal training that inhibits simplicity and grace of expression. (In fact I occasionally detect signs in myself — which in its way is probably as remarkable a feat of critical self-appraisal as that of a bore who occasionally suspects that even *he* might be one!) And if the average judicial opinion is the prosecution's star Exhibit A for the truth of this proposition, there is negative evidence even more impressive. Where are the poets, essayists, novelists and dramatists who have sprung from the law? A mere handful. And most of these, one suspects, escaped from bondage despite and not because of their legal backgrounds. Doctors, who presumably spent their student days with their eyes glued to the gizzard, come out far more handsomely.

The lawyer increasingly suffers too — as does everyone — from the modern curse of overspecialization. These days he has to read an enormous amount of assorted legal stuff to keep even moderately abreast of his profession. While this probably accounts, at least partly, for his reputation as being one of the poorest buyers and readers of general books — the poor guy is simply too pooped after all *that* to read anything more demanding than a whodunit or a newspaper — the dismal fact remains that the increasingly ingrown quality of his reading does little to improve his felicity of expression. Indeed, the pressures are quite the other way; he tends to get worse instead of better.

By the time he gets to be a judge the average lawyer is so far sunk in verbal sin that it would be little short of a miracle if his opinions were endurable reading let alone a pleasure to peruse. Good writing is never easy, heaven knows, and I suspect that much bad judicial writing springs from nothing more than plain carelessness mixed with a dash of arrogance, a simple failure to take adequate pains. Is it any mystery, then, that a judge's stuff comes out sounding so often like the dictated monstrosities of the average American businessman?

If pedestrian judicial opinions often result from a failure to take adequate pains, paradoxically a fussy taking of excessive pains spawns even more awesome and charmless specimens of the genre. "Peninhanders" I call these latter opinions because their perpetrators seem promptly to hemorrhage at the wrist and relapse into helpless rhetorical incontinence the moment they Take Pen in Hand. "Remember, you are now writing for Posterity," they seem to keep saying over and over. And posterity gets an earful.

Now the choice between careless writing and highfalutin writing may be narrow, but at least the former is free from the added vice of pretension. The slipshod writer may occasionally deviate into profundity and revelation, but ornate writing almost invariably masks shallowness of thought. So while there may be a ray of hope for the careless writer, the windbag almost never repents or runs down; like the tree toad, puffed to bursting, he croaks on and on, sustained and enchanted by the heavenly music of his own voice.

It is a curious fact, and also in a sense contradictory of some of the things I am saying, that much of the most refreshing judicial writing around these days comes from our busiest courts and judges. Is it that they don't have *time* to write badly? While their opinions may not often get embalmed in anthologies or quoted in style manuals, they are engagingly direct, clear and workmanlike, mercifully devoid of rhetorical garbage, and I have been happy to quote from a few in this book. (I am also happy to have just planted my escape hatch!)

One wearies so of the prevalence of murky and overblown judicial writing that it is easy to overstate one's case. I do not say or imply that we do not have excellent judges who can write like angels and who turn out opinions that are a joy and a delight. We do have, and I have luckily known some. My point and my puzzlement is that they are so few.

My concern is not only with the lumbering and inflated style of much judicial writing, bad as that is. The thing may be more serious. More disquieting is the gnawing suspicion that a thought or decision poorly expressed might come simply from poor thinking in the first place. Is it unforgivable heresy to suggest that in order for a judge to *say* a thing well he must first *think* it well? And that if he doesn't then maybe he hasn't? (I reject as esoteric nonsense McLuhan's recent assertion that "Clear prose indicates the absence of thought." Wouldn't the logic of this, if pursued, make the babble of idiots the profoundest utterances of men?) Equally disturbing is the feeling that the increasing remoteness and "privacy" of judicial language is resulting in a growing lack of communication with and alienation of our people from the law of their land.

Is there any cure? Damn' little, I'm afraid. For one thing our educators are themselves frequently among the worst offenders, suffering as so many do from a progressive and seemingly incurable speech impediment that might be called "academia." Yet in my more optimistic moments I sometimes feel that it might help if every law school in the land gave a rigorous pass-or-perish course in speaking and writing plainly. (And if many of their professors were made to attend.) But by then I suppose it is too late. Treatment should probably have started back in kindergarten.

While I wouldn't go quite as far as Robert Moses (but, then, who ever does?), who wrote recently that he would "settle . . . for any educational system . . . which teaches pupils to read, write and speak simple English," the old warrior clearly has something there; surely he probes a sore spot in our cultural pretensions. What price years of expensive schooling if we keep turning out educated mutes? And occasional mutes, moreover, who boldly find virtue in their mutehood?

In any case, while the law is not simple, heaven knows, I can see no compelling reason why it should not be discussed in plain English, and many reasons why it should. After all, the law may be our last best barrier between at least a pretense at civilization and outright anarchy. If so, perhaps the law has grown too important to be understood only by lawyers.

Now back to the salt mines.

II

Some Variations on an Ancient Theme

OLD Doc Parsons, for many years our town's busiest unlicensed abortioner, when once asked to define rape,
replied: "The wrong man." Others have defined it as the
depth of bad taste or again as conclusive proof that men truly
descended from monkeys, but these and other variant schools
of thought were overruled centuries ago by those old English
judges who, since at least the reign of Edward I in the twelfth
century, tersely defined rape as the carnal knowledge of a
woman by a man by force and without her consent. This ancient definition, with only slight variations, prevails in our law
down to the present day.

Nestling ever so innocently in the legal indices between
Railroads and Receivers, Rape has had a long, abundant and
dishonorable career. The extravagant lengths to which men
will go to satisfy their appetites and get themselves in trouble
is nowhere better illustrated than in this uneasy realm. In this
essay I shall explore a few odd byways in this dark forest of
the criminal law. Which brings me abruptly to Variation
Number One.

*Can a man legally be convicted of the rape of a sleeping
woman?*

Most laymen and sheltered lawyers (sheltered from the

criminal law, that is) would probably say no, the guttier or more compassionate among them probably adding that any man who couldn't arouse a woman to consciousness during such an encounter deserves condolence far more than criminal prosecution for his pains. They would be wrong; the books are crammed with cases where men were convicted — and stayed convicted — of raping unsuspecting women in their sleep.

Where the average layman goes wrong is in his natural assumption that the act of intercourse must be completed, brought to climax, and in his incredulity that even the most lethargic female could remain asleep through all that. The law says otherwise: that in rape *any* penetration, however slight, completes the offense, and that the act need not be consummated. In almost all of the cases consulted the woman *did* wake up and promptly raised a hue and cry, and the decisions are virtually uniform that this adds up to rape. But what if she wakes up and silently submits or, worse yet, joins in the undertaking? What then? The cases are sharply split — of which more presently.

In the past an unaccountably large proportion of these "sleeping" rape cases emanated from the state of Arkansas where, at one time at least, the sight of a sleeping woman evidently goaded its males to ecstasies of illicit passion. Pondering this phenomenon, one speculates that it might have sprung from the same atavistic impulse that made its people cling so long and wistfully to a man called Faubus and still cling to its ancient anti-evolution statute.* But perhaps this is to invest the thing with too much symbolism and primitive earth wisdom; maybe it was the only way the menfolk down there figured they wouldn't be talked out of the enterprise.

Yet a certain monotony is found in these old Arkansas

---

* A distinction it shares with Mississippi and Tennessee, but maybe not for long, as the Arkansas statute has recently been successfully attacked in a lower court there by a brave teacher.

rape cases involving sleeping women — the stalk, the discovered and invaded quarry, the subsequent hullabaloo — and for my illustrative case I instead turn to its sister state, Missouri, which has the distinction of spawning one of the classic cases in this field *(State of Missouri v. Welch).*

The Widow Dorrity, age forty-one, and her four children ranging from nine to sixteen, lived on her farm near Cushion Lake in New Madrid County. On a Saturday night in October, 1903, having had a hard day, she retired early and shortly went to sleep. With her in bed was her twelve-year-old daughter. In an adjoining bedroom one of her sons lay asleep with a visiting neighbor boy. Peace prevailed, but not for long.

During the night she suddenly awakened and found a man in bed with her. Then, to her horror, she discovered that not only was he in bed with her but on top of her and having intercourse with her. She tried to resist and push him away but, as she later testified, he persisted and overcame her resistance and, finishing his task, escaped through a bedroom window and then, in droll farewell, hurled a chunk of wood through the windowpane. She ran to the shattered window and looked out. In the bright moonlight she recognized John Welch, once a hired hand on her farm and then a blacksmith in a neighboring village.

She rounded up the children and, when all were dressed, set out for the Ike Grimes's farm about a mile away. There she told Mrs. Grimes what had happened, out of hearing of the children, and all of them spent the night there. The next morning she went to town and swore out a rape warrant against her former hired man John Welch. Upon his arraignment in circuit court he pleaded not guilty and the decks were cleared for the most sensational criminal trial ever held in New Madrid County.

The trial was long and bitter and the evidence violently contradictory and marked by much rebuttal and counterrebuttal. The Widow Dorrity took the stand and, in a low voice, told in detail her harrowing story. Yes, she had undressed and retired early that night with one of her daughters. She wore only a loose nightgown and guessed she usually slept on her back. When she awoke, she testified, the defendant was not only on her but was already having intercourse with her. She was firm on that point.

When the impatient defense lawyer had his chance at her on cross-examination, one of his first questions was: Why hadn't she pushed her attacker away? She had tried, she said, but she was a small woman, weighing barely over a hundred pounds, who had recently been ill, and moreover was then having her difficult menses, while he was a big powerful man. . . .

"Why didn't you scream?" was the next searching question.

She had tried to, she explained, but he had clutched her throat with one hand and held his other hand over her mouth.

"Why didn't you scream when he left your side?"

"I did," she answered calmly. "That is what aroused the children."

"Why didn't you tell them what happened?"

"Because it — it was not very nice talk to tell youngsters," she answered with downcast eyes.

"Why didn't you kick your daughter awake — the sleeping girl lying there right at your side?" was the next question.

"I don't know," she answered lamely. "I guess I never thought of it."

"Why, after his arrest and after he got out on bail, did you go to the defendant's blacksmith shop to have a saw sharpened?"

"That's a lie!" she replied heatedly. "I never saw or spoke to that man after that — that awful night. . . ."

"How can you be so sure that it was the *defendant* who did this to you? After all it was nighttime, wasn't it?"

"After he broke the window I ran to it and saw him standing there in the moonlight. I saw him plain. He worked and lived with us for six years. There is no mistake."

John Welch's main defense was an alibi; that is, not only that he didn't commit the act but that he was somewhere else at the time and couldn't possibly have done it. But he wasn't putting all his eggs in one defense basket and these clever questions asked of the Widow Dorrity on cross-examination by his lawyer were revealing yet another facet of his defense: namely, that even if the jury didn't quite swallow his alibi, he would subtly suggest to them either that the woman for some dark reason had made up her story or, alternatively, that she had not only consented to the intercourse but had cooperated in it — as shown by her action later in bringing a saw to him to be sharpened, presumably to acquaint him of her forgiveness and availability for a return bout. If only he could sow enough seeds of reasonable doubt . . .

"I didn't do it," the dour defendant Welch declared flatly when it came his turn to take the stand. "That night I worked late in my blacksmith shop by lantern light — workin' on a log wagon for Combs' mill. Then I went over to Ed Welbron's lunch room and et some oysters and then I went straight to my roomin' house and went to bed. I was awful tired, workin' late an' all."

Ed Welbron, purveyor of inland oysters, backed this up, testifying that he had earlier seen the defendant working in his nearby shop that night, drilling holes in some iron pieces by lantern light; that later he had come over to his lunchroom-grocery store and bought and ate some potted ham (whither oysters flown?), and then, quite late, started for his nearby roominghouse, saying he felt sleepy. "He looked awful tired."

In rebuttal the state put on more witnesses, some of whom testified that Ed Welbron had sold out and was no longer running his luncheon-grocery store in Stewart on the night in question and further that the "tired" defendant Welch had not worked or even been in his blacksmith shop that night. There was more rebuttal and counterrebuttal on both sides —

it was a savage no-holds-barred trial — and finally the lawyers made their impassioned arguments, the judge gave his
calm instructions, and the jury retired. They found John
Welch guilty of the rape of the Widow Dorrity. He promptly
appealed.

After reviewing the facts and much of the conflicting testimony, Mr. Justice Burgess plunged boldly into his main opinion: "To ravish [a favorite judicial euphemism for rape] a
woman is to have carnal connection [another favorite euphemism for sexual intercourse] with her forcibly and without
her consent. . . . If . . . [she] was asleep at the time, as
testified by her, she was, of course, incapable of giving assent."

Things were already looking bad for the defendant; His
Honor was begging the very question on which he based his
main hope. The judge then reviewed many of the older cases
where cohabitation with a sleeping woman was held to be
rape, quoting with approval from an old Texas case where it
was said, "The act of copulation by a man with a sleeping
woman, without her consent, is sufficient to constitute rape,
although the force used be only such as is necessary to the
mere act of copulation." The defendant was now down to his
final main contention, namely, that the woman's conduct
after awakening amounted to submission and consent, thus
vitiating any prior rape. Justice Burgess met this without hesi-
tation:

"She knew nothing about the assault and penetration of her
person until she awoke and found the defendant on her. . . .
After that no submission or consent . . . could avail the
defendant." His Honor conceded that the authorities were not
harmonious, but he chose to put his and Missouri's money on
Bishop's *New Criminal Law* where, approvingly quoting from
it, it was said: " 'The true view is believed to be that when the
offense has been completed by penetration, no remission by
the woman or consent by her, however quickly following, can
avail the man.' Judgment affirmed. All concur."

The exhausted blacksmith had exhausted his remedies and was on his way to prison.

What on earth makes men like Blacksmith Welch *do* things like this? As an ex-DA who has collided with perhaps more than his share of rape cases and rape defendants — though, I must confess, never with a "sleeper" — I venture a guess.

A powerful case can be made for the proposition that the average man sexually is a wandering untethered bull restrained mostly by pride and fear. But it is a pride that swells easily into reckless male vanity, a fear that melts swiftly in the hot flame of raw male desire. The massive male ego, especially when unencumbered by excessive brains or exhilarated by an injudicious blend of passion and bar whiskey, is easily convinced that any woman who lives alone — widow, grass widow, bachelor girl, whatever — is panting to get a man in bed with her, preferably himself. Intellectual giants of this stamp, and there are many, are quick to misinterpret the slightest cordiality — a passing nod, a civil greeting, a casual smile — as a seductively veiled invitation to come join them there. Real soon.

These hallucinated souls seem never to realize that any man who invades the bed of a woman who hasn't unmistakably invited him there is, among other things, a plain damn fool. They persist in their delusion despite abundant evidence to the contrary: the wealth of legal cases against them, the thousands of their deluded brothers languishing in prison, the disaster that must inevitably follow treating any woman as though she were a bitch in heat. That these men are mostly stupid, crude, ego-sodden and utterly repellent is undeniable. Yet I can't help wondering whether they should ever be equated with the true pathological rapist.

One need not set up shop as a lay analyst to guess that the two are not identical. One is mostly an egocentric idiot, the other a dangerously sick psychopath. One fatuously deludes himself he can charm or sneak his way in; the other resolutely shuns acquiescence and submission and is apt to become impotent in its presence. One is a sneak thief of love, the other a hold-up man. The one tends to run when the going gets rough; the other lusts after terror and resistance. To the true rapist, risk, violence and imminent danger, far from deterring him, are all part of the attraction.

But how can the poor surprised woman know what kind of interloper she has on her hands? She can't, of course, but the authorities can later, when prosecution and punishment are in order. Possibly there should be degrees of rape or some in-between crime to fit the plain damn fools. I do not wish to be misunderstood. I make no plea that these gristle-headed bed invaders should go free and not be punished. I suggest only that possibly they should not be treated or punished in the same way as pathological rapists. For one thing, to do so doubtless encourages many juries to let them go entirely when they have no appropriate alternative other than traditional rape. Simple assault and battery — the usual alternative — scarcely fills the bill. It's a large and perplexing subject.

More akin to the true rapist is the daring soul who invades the bed of a sleeping woman, the bed also being occupied by her sleeping husband or lover. There are a surprising number of such cases, so many, in fact, that one wonders what the intruding defendant deserves most: a medal for his heroism or a psychiatrist for his head. If the lone-woman artist risks disaster, the three-in-a-bedder clamors for it. Most "normal" males would be so terrified they could never get on with the festivities. Yet in a recent West Coast "sleeper" case, so devoted to his work was the intruder that when the woman awoke and aroused her sleeping husband lying beside her, the latter had to go get a carving knife and chase the intent defendant away with it.

True, the surly blacksmith in Widow Dorrity's case did rough up his victim some — grabbing her throat, as she said, to prevent her from yelling — but this is not typical of most of the lone-woman "sleeper" artists, who, as I have suggested, might be called the sneak thieves of the baffling world of rape. Which gets me back to the court's opinion in this old Missouri case.

As a penetrating judicial analysis and exposition of the *why* of the rule — that the post-awakening deportment of the woman cannot relate back and purge the "sleeping" rape — the opinion is a frost; guilt was affirmed more by incantation than by cerebration. While the reasoning may be faulty, the message is loud and clear: "Stay to hell out and off of strange beds and strange ladies, Buster! If you're caught you'll be found guilty of rape, regardless of what the lady does when she awakes, because we *say* you're guilty!" Most litigants — including criminal defendants — are far more concerned with what courts hold than why they hold it; they rather wisely suspect that being sent to prison even in the flawless syllogisms of a Socrates doesn't make the sentence any easier to serve.

Yet in neighboring Iowa the rule is — or at least was — precisely the opposite: that the sleeping "rape" may be purged and disappear unless the woman upon awakening puts up all the resistance she can. In an old case that, emotionally at least, simply cried out for guilt, the Iowa supreme court let the male invader go (*Pollard v. State*). Presumably the oyster-eating blacksmith would have been decorated had he felt strong enough that night to get across the border.

The Pollards, husband and wife, slept on the fateful night in the same bedroom with her twelve-year-old sister. During the night the roving husband crept into the younger girl's bed and woke her by having intercourse with her. As she later testified at his trial for rape, she was awakened by the pleasure of the act; she felt no particular pain, but nevertheless she asked him to go away, whereupon he told her to keep still, that he would not hurt her. Convicted at his jury trial, the defendant appealed the refusal of the trial judge to give a requested jury instruction that if she had not resisted any more than she testified he should be acquitted. The supreme court bought this argument, reversing the conviction. What happened, the court said, "is just as consistent with willingness as with unwillingness, and takes its character from subsequent [to awakening] events."

So that the decision isn't made to look any worse than it is — which is quite bad enough — it should in fairness be added that Iowa was then doubtless operating under the old common-law age limit of ten, below which the consent of the female is no defense to rape. By statute that limit has since been sharply raised in virtually all states, including Iowa — in some to as high as eighteen. This harsh old *Pollard* case might have been one of the reasons for it. That a mature woman upon awakening might so act or fail to act that the initial intercourse ceases to be rape and dissolves in consent is at least an arguable legal proposition; but that so sophisticated a test should be applied coldly to the confused reactions of a cowed and palpitant child is to mock both the rule and the judicial process itself. Old as the case is, it still stinks.

In a few of the earlier cases in this field of "sleeping" rape guilt or innocence sometimes depended on semantic distinctions almost metaphysical in their refinement. As noted earlier, the common law and most statutes early defined rape simply as the carnal knowledge of a woman by a man by force and without her consent. But some legislators, with their apparently helpless occupational passion for florid and redundant utterance, saw fit to tinker with the old definition; they either substituted "against her will" in place of the old words "without her consent" or with a fine Spencerian flourish tacked it on at the end. Still others used "against her consent" in place of the old "without her consent."

Intruders upon sleeping women should have thanked these legislative tinkerers because a number of courts in such jurisdictions thereupon held that these changes made it no rape because the new words "against her consent (or will)" implied a conscious and communicated rejection of the engagement by the woman — "No, *no,* NO!" — which a sleeping woman manifestly could not have or give. But these few early decisions must be regarded as aberrations in the law; nowadays virtually all courts nail all intrepid intruders upon sleeping women, whatever the deviant wording of the statute — this by indulging in the not wholly unwarranted assumption that a sleeping woman no more "consents" to the invasion of her person by an intruding stranger than she is deemed to consent if, while sleeping, he crept into her bedroom and stole her purse from under her pillow.

If virtually all American courts, then, are now agreed that if a man invades the bed of a sleeping woman and has intercourse with her, it is rape, they still remain sharply split on what happens if, when she awakes — as she usually does — she does not *immediately* resist and raise appropriate hell. (This is the defense picture Blacksmith Welch was trying so hard to paint in his case and which finally got the brother-in-law off in the old Iowa case.) Some courts hold with Missouri that it doesn't make any difference what she later does — that the rape is over with and the man is guilty; others, that if upon awakening she does not sufficiently resist, the intercourse ceases to be rape. Put tersely: if she hollers, rape it remains; if she hugs, rape turns into romance.

There is something to be said for both views. On the guilty side is a natural reluctance of the courts to reward the bold interloper by allowing him to profit by any reciprocal passion he may so illicitly have aroused in a sleep-befuddled woman. Moreover, these courts imply, this raiding of strange beds is dangerous and socially intolerable and must be put down at any cost. Finally, since most women get little time to rehearse their reactions upon awakening to find an unknown man in bed having intercourse with them, the marauding male should scarcely benefit from *anything* the woman might do or fail to do.

On the innocent side there is an implicit feeling in the cases going that way that rape being one of our gravest crimes, still punishable by death in some jurisdictions, no man should lightly be convicted of it. Possibly a little empathy is at work: there but for the grace of God . . . Judges express themselves rather gingerly on this subject (are they afraid of their super-supreme-courts at home?) but ever so delicately implied in some of these "innocence" cases is a philosophical assumption that men and women have been sacking up together, with varying degrees of informality and reluctance, for an awful long time now — with the prospects bright for a continuation of the tradition — and that if the misguided male didn't physically harm or threaten her, and she was big enough and old enough and appeared to be none the worse for her experience, or even enjoyed it, why make a "federal case" out of it?

The main trouble with any rigid rule on the subject is that it is hard to find one that can encompass all the ramifications of such a situation and still do justice in every case. When a sleeping woman awakes in the middle of the night to find an unknown man in bed and aboard her, who can dare say with confidence what her reaction will or should be? A sheltered judge who at the time was playing poker over at the Elks Club? To make it rape, must she possibly risk her life defending a virtue which by hypothesis has already flown? The decided cases show that her unrehearsed responses may range from the most violent indignation and resistance through passive acceptance on to unbridled rapture over such a delightful and flattering surprise.

Yet a whore can raise the most magnificent hue and cry, delivered in matchless Billingsgate, while a virgin's silence or even her apparent cooperation may stem from nothing more than sheer terror or a despairing acquiescence, the more quickly to get the nightmare over with. What judge-made rule can fit all the wild mixture of emotions going on here? Why must guilt or innocence be determined solely by relative poutings and squirmings or by measuring shrill female decibels? Where does justice lie?

This is where the Anglo-American jury system so often

comes to the rescue. As a battered ex-DA I have smarted over lost cases (including rape cases) that at the time I thought I clearly should have won — and vice versa. But now that those tumultuous days are over and peace has descended, I find I have a sneaking suspicion that most of those old juries did the "right" thing in most of their cases, whatever my stung feelings at the time. In retrospect I have more and more been struck by the surprising capacity of ordinary jurors — plasterers, painters, bartenders, housewives, iron miners — to penetrate the darkest recesses of the human psyche, astonished by their amazing sensitivity to the most delicate nuances of human behavior. Although I never prosecuted one, in these "sleeping" rape situations I rather think that by some kind of indefinable mental osmosis they can generally tell whether the gentleman is a bum or the lady is a tramp.

The subject does not lend itself to dogmatism and I do not wish to overstate it. Heaven knows there have been many cases where jurors have been awesomely wrong when they failed to get "right" instructions — and in still other cases even when they *did*, as this book richly demonstrates. I mean simply that in cases depending upon a correct appraisal of human deportment and basic human drives and emotions, in situations lying within the ken of their experience or observation (this reservation is important), the average jury is more likely to come up with a "right" verdict than a wrong one. If this sounds too mystic and Cloud Seventeenish perhaps I remained district attorney for too long. Or maybe I should blame my old friend Judge Bell.

This grand and wise old circuit judge, the one and only Frank A. Bell, once said to me when I was a green young DA still smarting over the loss of a bitter murder case: "Remember, son, jurors in all criminal cases ask themselves two big questions: 'Is the son-of-a-bitch guilty? If so, do we want to see him punished?' It is the answer to this last question that you've got to learn to live with."

I now think Judge Bell was right and perhaps that is why I

can't fret too much over these sharply conflicting rules in the law of "sleeping" rape or anything else; I can't because I still cling to the notion that in "human nature" cases most jurors will somehow come up with the "right" verdicts, whatever erudite judges tell them is the law. One of the glories of the Anglo-American legal system is that our lay juries keep us frequently overtrained and underexposed judges and lawyers from stealing the law away from the people. But maybe I'm just an unreconstructed old jury buff who should shut up and get on with the next variation.

Can a man legally be convicted of the rape of his own wife?

You have doubtless learned your lesson now and will probably slyly answer yes. This time you will be right but quite probably for the wrong reasons. No case has been found anywhere in which a husband has been convicted of the sole active rape of his own lawful wife. That was decided centuries ago when Lord Hale laid down the proposition in a quaint dictum in which he said: "But the husband cannot be guilty of a rape committed by himself upon his lawful wife, for by their mutual matrimonial consent and contract the wife hath given up herself in this kind unto her husband, which she cannot retract." And this has been the uniform rule in the United States ever since an old Massachusetts decision handed down in 1857.

Lord Hale's dictum to the contrary, there have been a few successful prosecutions in this country against a husband for giving his wife a venereal disease or for enforced acts of sexual perversion with her. These were not rape cases, however, but rather prosecutions for some form of assault or under special statutes defining and prohibiting acts of gross indecency and the like. The only hint found anywhere recognizing the possibility of a husband's guilt as a prime actor of a rape upon his own wife occurs in a fairly recent English case where the wife had previously obtained a judicial separation (not divorce) order providing among other things that she need no longer cohabit with her husband. The court ventured a cautious dictum that in these circumstances the husband might be guilty of a rape upon his own wife.

But while a husband may, without criminal liability for rape, physically force himself sexually upon his wife regardless of her wishes, he may not lawfully force intercourse upon her by another man. And if he does so he may be equally guilty of rape along with the other man. Again dependable old Lord Hale's measured tones must be heeded:

"A. the husband of B. intends to prostitute her to a rape by C. against her will, and C. accordingly doth ravish her, A. being present, and assisting to this rape: in this case these points were resolved, 1. That this was a rape in C. notwithstanding the husband assisted in it, for tho in marriage she hath given up her body to her husband, she is not to be by him prostituted to another. 2. That the husband being present, aiding and assisting, is also guilty as a principal in rape, and therefore, altho the wife cannot have an appeal of rape against her husband; yet he is indictable for it at the king's suit as a principal. 3. That in this case the wife may be a witness against her husband, and accordingly she was admitted, and A. and C. were both executed."

So much for A. and C. They did things with dispatch back in those days.

His Lordship cited as his authority for his proposition *Lord Audley's Case,* decided in 1631, where the gallant husband, having forced his wife to submit to intercourse with his servant, was held guilty of rape. So we see that not only may a husband in this way be held guilty of the rape of his own wife, albeit obliquely, but there have even been cases that have held him guilty of rape even though he might in fact be sexually impotent.

All of which brings us down to the *Chapman* case, decided in Michigan not long after the Civil War, and perhaps not excessively described by one of the indignant justices who sat on it as "the foulest of crimes," and he added that a case "seldom occurs in a community showing more depravity in the accused, or a greater outrage to common decency and public morals." Since the case is not only one of the most bizarre I have encountered (and also one of the saddest), as well as one of the earliest in America holding the husband equally guilty of rape along with the man he puts up to it, we will take a look at it.

Back in 1881, some months before the case broke, the defendant, Jerry Chapman, seduced a thirteen-year-old girl called Maggie Smith. Having got her pregnant, and presumably to avoid the perils of a prosecution for statutory rape (that is, any intercourse whatever, voluntary or not, with a female child under the prevailing age of consent) he got her to lie about her age and married her. Rapidly tiring of both the state of Maggie and that of matrimony, he then dreamed up a wild scheme to get rid of her. As part of his scheme he got a drifter called Reagan to come live with them as a star boarder. Plans were laid, the stage set.

As part of his grotesque plan the husband, Jerry Chapman, secretly (to Maggie, that is) bored some holes through the bedroom wall so that he could watch the proceedings when the time arrived. Came the big day, the defendant and his brother Oscar took up their stations at the strategic peepholes, while the drifter Reagan advanced upon the unsuspecting Maggie in her bedroom — a rare kind of Restoration cum Mack Sennett farce if it hadn't been so deadly. At first Reagan, who knew all along he was being watched, tried the manly arts of seduction, but plucky Maggie rejected him scornfully. Masculine wile failing he caught her by the throat and threw her down and, while she vainly tried to fight him off and equally vainly shrieked for help, had his way with her, as they used to say in the ladies' magazines. At the climax of this drama the husband and his brother Oscar burst into the bedroom, the husband shouting, "Now I have caught you!"

In due course the broken Maggie dragged her way to the

sheriff and told her story and the drifter Reagan was promptly arrested, charged with, and convicted of rape. But the countryside still remained up in arms over the atrocity and, the clamor growing even more deafening, the red-faced authorities next arrested Jerry Chapman and his brother Oscar, charging them also with the rape of Maggie Chapman, this under a statute, long common in most states, making all persons aiding, assisting or abetting in a crime equally guilty as principals. The two brothers stood mute, pleas of not guilty were entered on their behalf, and Wayne County (the Detroit area) braced itself for perhaps the most sensational criminal trial in its not-unsensational history.

Maggie appeared and again told her story: How Reagan had come into the bedroom and forced his attentions upon her; how she had rejected them; how he had then grabbed her and thrown her down and raped her; of her vain screams for help and how later her husband had burst in with his triumphant accusations. She told how, when she saw her husband and rushed up to him exclaiming, "Oh, dear, kill him!" he coldly pushed her away and the three men shortly left the house together, apparently on friendly terms. She then told how three days later she was served with divorce papers filed by her husband on the grounds of the adultery of his wife with Reagan.

The hapless Reagan was brought to court out of prison by the prosecution to tell his strange story, and it boiled down to this: That the husband Jerry Chapman had solicited him, Reagan, to come board at his house, and bargained that if the husband could catch Reagan in bed or, better yet, "aboard of her," in Reagan's words (so that the husband could accordingly get rid of her by divorcing her for adultery) Reagan would be paid $25; that one fine day after the peepholes were bored and the brothers were at their stations and Reagan alerted that the stage was set, he went in and raped the wife; that the husband and his brother witnessed the rape and heard the wife's screams and watched her struggles without lifting a hand and that (as the wife had already testified) at the crucial moment the two brothers burst into the bedroom, the husband exclaiming, "Now I have caught you!"

The state's evidence in, the defendant husband took the stand and flatly denied everything. He said that no such bargain had ever been made with Reagan, but that on the contrary, he being jealous and suspicious of his wife, he and his brother hid in the house to verify his growing mistrust; that Maggie Chapman was a willing participant in the adultery with — not rape by — Reagan; and that when he rushed into the room during the adultery he grabbed and brandished a chair, shouting: "I have caught you now right in the act — I have a notion to paralyze both of you." Loyal brother Oscar stoutly supported this testimony.

The evidence in, the prosecutor in his jury argument scornfully pointed out that within three days after the commission of whatever actually took place the defendant had indeed filed his bill of complaint for divorce on the ground of adultery; and that at no time did he lay a hand on Reagan or seek to prosecute him for rape or prosecute both of them for the crime of adultery. The jury arguments in, the judge instructed the jury, which retired and had a smoke and whatever else they do out there, and presently came back and through their foreman declared they found the husband Jerry Chapman guilty of the rape of his wife Maggie. The husband promptly appealed to the state supreme court.

There Chapman's astute lawyer argued that even if his client had made any such bargain with Reagan (which the husband at all times had resolutely denied) it was not for rape but for adultery, and that his mere presence in another room could not make him guilty of Reagan's independent and unplanned crime; that to be found guilty he would have had to manifest some positive act of assistance in the actual rape — of which there was no shred of evidence.

In a scalding opinion Justice Morse rejected all of these arguments, His Honor conceding that "the mere presence of a person when a murder or a rape is being committed, without any previous agreement or conspiracy . . . will not [make him] . . . guilty . . . although by his interference he might have prevented it. . . ."

"But the case at bar is one in which aid and assistance were rendered. . . . Reagan knew [the husband] . . . was in the next room, in sight of his work; and when the wife screamed, and respondent did not interfere, he knew that the husband was willing he should succeed [by any means and thus] . . . imparted to him a confidence in his under-taking. . . . By the lifting of a finger or the opening of his mouth he could have prevented the injury to his wife, but he did not do so."

The judge paused and continued scornfully: "A husband who could barter with another for the despoiling of his wife's virtue, and stand by to witness it with his brother, and remain passive and silent while such object was obtained by violence, and then use such permitted and encouraged rape to divorce her from him, and by this, and perjury added, publish her to the world as an adulteress, is morally guilty of as foul a crime as can be named in the calendar. The offense of Reagan, heinous as it is, sinks into insignificance beside it."

The judge continued to pour it on: "His bargain with Reagan was to fix it so that he could catch Reagan 'in bed with or aboard of her' " — as Reagan had colorfully phrased it during his testimony. In the judge's view, if Reagan was wronged, it was the jury who wronged him.

At this juncture in this fantastic case occurred one of those courtroom events that sometimes tempts one to despair of the whole judicial process: after all these indignant fulminations a majority of the supreme court did an abrupt about-face and let Chapman go on a technicality — that certain witnesses at the preliminary examination in justice court had not at its conclusion signed their testimony! Justice Sherwood all but screamed his dissent.

In a vibrant, blistering opinion he called the defendant husband everything but one of Nature's ignoblemen, exhausting all the then current genteel legal euphemisms (to which I, when a judge, added a few of my own) for calling a man a prime, genuine, unreconstructed, nonreturnable, four-alarm, five-karat, six-ply bastard. "Who is this man that so plaintively inquires whether technical justice has been done him?" he demanded scathingly. "In my judgment a case seldom occurs in a civilized community showing more depravity in the accused, or more outrage to common decency or public morals. It is hard to conceive of an act more cruel . . . to the young wife, whose person, pride and chastity were violated and mangled, and whose hope, happiness, and very life have been essentially destroyed, than was perpetrated by this villainous defendant, who is now pleading for the advantage . . . [that] . . . a technical construction . . . of the law [may give] . . . him in avoiding . . . his crime."

Alas, the good justice might have saved both his rhetoric and his wind; the defendant Jerry Chapman was let go, presumably divorced his shattered child-wife and, one almost prays, lived for one hundred and eight more years — with one sleepless eye glued relentlessly to a peephole, watching other men endlessly pleasuring themselves.

It would be pleasant to think that Chapman was the last male in this country who ever assisted or conspired to have a stranger rape his wife — pleasant but sadly erroneous. There have been many similar cases since then, including one recent one in Oklahoma so revolting ("revoluting," His Honor Justice of the Peace Willy Sharp used to say), so overripe, so utterly appalling in its incredible details that to include it in a book of general circulation might bar it from the mails. It makes even Brother Chapman look good.

In a fairly recent Texas case a white husband, also wanting to get rid of his wife, bargained with a Negro to rape her while he composed himself in a tree and watched the Negro drag his wife out of the house and forcibly have at her. (This time the conviction stuck, as it also did in an even more recent West

Virginia case involving precisely the same situation.) Lest I be suspected of sectional bias I may add that our northern states have contributed some equally Dostoevskian dandies to this unlovely branch of the law of rape.

But the case that really stops the clock is a weird old North Carolina one (1890) where the white husband held a loaded gun over his white wife and a Negro and ordered them on pain of death to cohabit in his presence. The terrified Negro reluctantly tried to follow orders but out of fright failed to perform. Then, when the brandished gun went off in the hands of the frenzied husband, the Negro fled in terror.

Both the Negro and the husband were arrested, *both* were charged with assault with intent to commit rape, and *both* were convicted — whereupon the husband alone appealed to the state supreme court, where his conviction was affirmed in an opinion that explicitly and tacitly affirmed the unappealed conviction of the Negro as well.

I first ran across this strange case in synopsis form in the *American Law Reports,* and for a time planned merely to devote a few passing lines to it as just another odd case. But the decision haunted me from the start and I made the following cryptic notes on it. "Lousy dec. Shd. have sprung Uncle and got after Legree for agg. assault vs. both. Maybe Cols. scared they'd lose Simon? Get & rd. this weirdee." Translated this means: "Lousy decision. Authorities should have let Negro go and prosecuted the husband alone for some form of aggravated assault against both the wife and the Negro. Maybe these outraged southern judges (Colonels — get it?) were afraid they'd lose the husband if they didn't also nail the Negro. Get and read the full text of this dreadful decision."

I did just that and my wonderment and depression increased, if possible, after reading the majority opinion, a long rambling thing that invoked the shade of Lord Hale, trotted out good old *Lord Audley's Case* and the old criminal-law writers Wharton and Bishop, along with impressive quotations from Broom's *Legal Maxims* and Blackstone's *Com-*

mentaries. All this was interlarded with layers of legalistic Latin, like a vast store-window birthday cake, the whole glittering edifice crowned with rhetorical candles glowing to the eternal sanctity of Womanhood and against the horrors of "violating female virtue." The opinion reads in fact like an early exercise in twentieth-century totalitarian dialectic, so helplessly Pavlovian in its response, so ostentatiously syllogistic, so blandly acrawl with legal non sequiturs, all building to a conclusion so awesomely wrong. It is like something out of Orwell's *1984* written a century earlier.

This chilling case has haunted me ever since I found and read it and I almost wish I hadn't, it seems so riddled with all the flyblown fantasies of high chivalry and vanished glory and galloping gallantry by which so many of our people still profess to live. And it is so incredibly cruel. The dubious rationale behind the decision seems to boil down to this:

Even then, there had been a number of dicta and several decisions that said that the husband could not be convicted in these circumstances if the actual perpetrator had already been or is acquitted; this on the fairly sound legal ground that where once it has been judicially established that the wife has *not* been raped the husband can scarcely be convicted as an accessory-principal to an offense that has officially been held not to have occurred.

Such an actual case is *State v. Haines,* where the husband held his wife down by her throat while his pal had his innings. The pal being first acquitted of rape in a separate jury trial, upon appeal the husband's later jury rape conviction was reversed for the reasons above noted. Interestingly enough, this very case suggests by way of dictum that if the husband had forced both the wife and the pal to cohabit, the husband alone might have been convicted of rape. If a case so decided exists it has eluded me in my research. But back to our main case.

From here it requires little cerebration to speculate that the outraged North Carolina court — outraged at what one of its own kind had made happen to his white wife at the hands of a Negro — so much wanted to punish the husband for his betrayal of [white] "female virtue" (and still look reasonably good legally) that it conveniently shut its eyes to the obvious law of the case and to the nightmarish plight of the terrified Negro, who instead became a thoughtless legal pawn to be casually sacrificed in the name of pride and honor.

Don't you see? They felt they couldn't let the Negro off, despite his obvious helplessness and lack of criminal intent, because then they mightn't be able to reach through him to their real goal, that dreadful white betrayer. But the really horrifying thing about the decision and the opinion is that the fate of the helpless Negro apparently meant so little to them; their only seeming concern with him was one of ill-restrained petulance that he had, however unwittingly, presented them with such a sticky legal problem. It is almost as though they were willing to see him punished for *that* as much as anything else.

That the Negro should have been prosecuted at all in these circumstances, let alone convicted, and his conviction approved by the highest court of his state, is hugely dismaying. I repeat: The only one who should have been prosecuted was the crazed husband, and this for some form of aggravated assault upon *both* his wife and the Negro. But no, the smilax and waffle-iron syndrome prevailed; a Woman's Sacred Honor had been sullied, sir, and law and common sense would have to be abdicated — and one terrified Negro allowed to vanish with the wind — while the good old chivalric code was preserved.

I consider this case altogether the worst and most frightening miscarriage of justice I have encountered among the hundreds of cases I have run across during the research for this book; worse, if possible, than the old Michigan *Chapman* case. It is not only bad law, but perverted law — perverted to the uses of passion and prejudice. It is bad enough to let the guilty go; to punish the innocent is infinitely worse. The only way this decision could possibly have been any worse — dreadful thought — is if they had not only held the Negro to his wrong conviction, which they did, but let the husband go.

The only redeeming feature about this whole dismal case is that one of the North Carolina judges — Merrimon, bless him — had the guts to rebel against the majority view and dissent from this wrong-headed and fantastic result. And he did so for precisely the same reasons that I did from a mere casual reading of a brief synopsis of the case: no criminal intent on the part of the Negro, and further that the husband alone should have been prosecuted for some form of aggravated assault against *both* the wife and the Negro. I tell this now not to show what a smart legal cookie I am, but rather to show how swiftly any moderately savvy lawyer — indeed any half-awake first-year student in Crimes — would see what a dreadful decision this is and penetrate so readily to what *should* have been done.

In his withering dissent Judge Merrimon, unlike the majority, didn't spout any Latin or invoke any old English Lords, or recite any odes to sacred female virtue, or indeed cite a single case. But, again unlike his Brothers, he thought and acted like a lawyer, he remembered his judicial oath and integrity, and he dared follow his own conscience.

But enough, enough. Listen to courageous Judge Merrimon: "[This case] . . . does not . . . warrant . . . a misapplication of well-established principles of criminal law. . . . The husband himself cannot ravish his own wife . . . he can only [do so] . . . by procuring, aiding, abetting or encouraging another to do so. In this case the negro" — lower case, of course, back in good ol' 1890 — "did not . . . rape . . . the wife nor did he assault her with such intent. . . . There was a total absence of such intent on his part. Then . . . how can the defendant be charged with . . . [the offense]? As the negro committed no assault with intent to commit rape, so the defendant did not. It is

said, Shall the defendant go quit [free]? Has he committed
no offense?"

But *who* had ever said the defendant might go quit? Obviously his Brothers privately had said so, of course. Don't you
see how clearly the cat is now out of the bag! This rhetorical
question reveals that the rest of the court knew (or thought
they knew) they had to burn the Negro to reach the husband
and also that Justice Merrimon had been unable privately to
dissuade them from their vengeful course. Watch him tersely
put them down:

"Most unquestionably he [the husband] shall not go quit.
He is chargeable with an assault upon his wife with a deadly
weapon, and with intent to kill, and a like assault upon the
negro. . . . [That the punishment for this offense may not
be adequate] . . . is no argument. . . . But what punishment would be? . . . [In any case] The [appellate] courts
have nothing to do with the punishment of offenders."

Here one can almost hear him sigh with weariness and res-
ignation as he abruptly concludes: "I will not pursue the subject further."

We now proceed to another variation with a final bravo to
the memory of Chief Justice Merrimon.

*Can a woman legally be convicted of the rape of another
woman?*

Now that you have successfully passed the bar, so to
speak, and grown wary of facile answers to *any* legal question, you are less likely to cry, *"Impossible!"* and might even
be tempted to say yes. In this you would be well advised;
again the ayes have it. In this area the law can do what nature
can't do; it can resourcefully transcend the bounds of physio-
logical possibility; a woman *can* be found guilty of the rape of
another woman, and in fact many have been.

She can for precisely the same reasons that a husband can
and has. The husband is held, as we have just seen, not be-

cause he is a husband but despite it; he is held, just as any stranger might be, on the theory that the aider and abetter is now almost universally held equally guilty as principal by case law or statute. So too with a woman. I'll now unveil a scorching case to prove it.

Frank Carter and Christine Griffith had been living together for many years. They were never married. At the time of the alleged offense they occupied a small four-room frame shack near the outskirts of Tempe, Arizona. Living with them in this shack was Betty, aged fifteen, Christine's daughter by another man.

On a January night in 1946 a Mrs. Zam happened temporarily to be staying in the house, evidently sleeping in the same room with the daughter Betty. During the night Frank Carter called out from his bedroom to his paramour's daughter, ordering her to come join him. The girl pretended not to hear him. He called again and again but still she did not come. Presently the girl's mother, Christine Griffith, came to Betty's bedroom and admonished her to heed Frank's call. The girl then reluctantly answered the shouted summons and it soon became evident to everyone in the flimsy thin-walled shack that the two — the man and the girl — were having sexual intercourse.

While the report does not clearly say so, it is also evident that it was the horrified transient guest, Mrs. Zam, who spread the word as soon as she could to the authorities. Frank Carter and Christine Griffith were arrested and both charged with the crime of statutory rape of her daughter Betty. At their trial it came out that Betty had been Frank Carter's mistress ever since she was thirteen. (The statutory age of consent in Arizona is eighteen, below which any intercourse is rape.) While again it is not made clear from the report, it appears that Mrs. Zam was a key witness for the prosecution. In her own testimony the embarrassed daughter Betty tried to shield her mother and excuse her conduct by saying that her first intercourse with Carter, when she was thirteen, had occurred without her mother's knowledge, presence or consent and that later she and her mother had bowed to Carter's frequent demands simply to keep peace in the home.

The jury was unimpressed; both Carter and the girl's mother were convicted and each given sizzling sentences to prison of from twenty to twenty-five years. Both appealed on numerous grounds, the mother on the additional ground that in the nature of things a female cannot ever be convicted of rape. After quoting the applicable Arizona statutes the court scuttled this argument almost laconically: "The answer to this contention is that by [our statutes] the distinction between principals and accessories before the fact is abolished. . . . [This makes our law] in accord with the general rule that 'a woman who aids, assists, procures, or counsels a man in the commission of rape is [equally] guilty of the offense. . . .' "

Had I been obliged to defend this unsavory case I think I would have been tempted to argue on appeal that any people who carried on this way, and especially in front of strangers (Mrs. Zam), were not so much immoral as totally amoral — sort of morally insane, as it were — and so could not possibly realize the gravity of their offenses, and that accordingly for such moral waifs their sentences were cruelly excessive. As a matter of fact, their lawyers did just that, but the supreme court said that such a determination (whether or not they were moral dwarfs) was up to the trial judge; that he had had a good chance to observe them at their trial and that apparently he had concluded that they really knew better. While conceding that "the law . . . contemplates that no cruel or unusual punishment shall be visited on anyone, including a person ignorant of the commonly accepted code of morals through no fault of his own and unaware of his nonconformity," the court rather smugly added, "Oftentimes such a person has to be confined for the protection of himself and society." The defendants lost their appeal.

But whether this curious behavior was immoral or amoral,

we now see that not only may a woman be convicted of the rape of another woman but, even more outré, a mother of her own daughter. Most of the cases in this field, while sordid enough, are fortunately not quite *this* sordid. Most involve the dreary efforts of madams or recruiting agents for houses of prostitution to enlist young girls to feed the ravening maw of the world's oldest profession.

One final side comment on this depressing case. That in stating the foregoing facts I may have appeared gingerly and a little vague, qualifying so many statements with "evidently" and "apparently" and the like, is not due to nicety or excessive prudery on my part, heaven forbid, but rather to the corresponding factual vagueness in the opinion I am drawing on. Which brings me to another interesting facet of the law: that many if not most judges, when confronted with "sensational" cases, particularly those involving sex, seem figuratively to flutter their eyelashes and purse their lips and lift their gowns and indulge in dainty euphemisms and generally carry on as though they were being forced to explain where babies come from to a class of three-year-olds. It would be rather amusing if it weren't so annoying to a person trying impersonally to state the facts upon which a grave rule of law is presumably based. To gloss over or omit salient facts, however repugnant they may be, is to cloud the law of a case and, worse yet, weaken it as precedent. But maybe I am only saying that even judges — as well as some toiling authors, alas — are not immune to occasional fits of muddy writing.

Can a man legally be convicted of the rape of a woman who erroneously thinks he is her husband?

This time the answer is neither Yes or No but Maybe. It all depends. Once again definition is in order, and so I repeat that the classical definition of rape requires that the intercourse be accomplished by force and without the consent of the woman. In states where this traditional definition still prevails (which includes most of them) there can be no rape where consent is given by the woman even though the man actively and fraudulently impersonates her husband. New York and Missouri seem to be among the few exceptions. It is the lack of force that saves the man in these situations, and it is usually said that his fraud upon the woman does not supply it.

England, after uncharacteristically floundering back and forth in some early cases, seems for the moment at least to accord with the majority American view that fraud in obtaining consent will not supply the necessary force to make the collision rape.

While not precisely on our question (that is, where the woman erroneously thinks the man is her husband) the English court in the famous (or infamous) Choirmaster case held that, where a choirmaster during a private tutoring session with a sixteen-year-old girl who sang in his choir, had intercourse with her by telling her that "I am going to make an air passage. This is my method of training. Your breathing is not quite right," his conviction for rape was proper. Presumably today he might go free; back then both his timing and his taste were equally faulty.

Ireland has long rejected the prevailing Anglo-American view that a consent to intercourse obtained by fraud or impersonation is a consent that bars rape, and as early as 1884 convicted its first husband-impersonator. By late dictum (1958) Australia seems to be falling in line with the Irish view.

In a 1926 Missouri case the conviction for rape of a physician who had intercourse with a woman patient under the pretext of giving her necessary medical treatment was affirmed, the court saying: "If it is rape . . . for a man to have illicit sexual connection with a woman while she is asleep and incapable of consenting, when no more force is used than is necessary to effect penetration . . ." — remember the old Blacksmith Welch case? — "we are unable to see why it is not also rape for a man to have [intercourse] . . .

through surprise, when she is awake, but utterly unaware of his [true] intention. . . . In such case the woman is incapable of consenting, because she has no [more] opportunity to give consent than has a sleeping woman."

The court then soared off on a broad dictum which indicates that, if the case ever arises there, Missouri might well join those very few states that hold (under common-law concepts of rape) husband-impersonators guilty of rape: "There is just as much reason to hold the [defendant physician] . . . guilty of rape . . . as there is where he commits the act while the woman is . . . asleep, or where . . . she submits . . . thinking such person to be her husband."

Missouri then might be regarded as a "sled-length" state to be avoided by artful seducers. In effect it says, and with considerable persuasiveness, that consent to intercourse obtained by this sort of fraud is no consent at all, because the comprehending intellect has not consented, only the deceived body; that what the woman in this case consented to was an act of medical treatment, not an act of sexual intercourse, which was never in her mind. From here it is just a step from saying that, in impersonation cases, what the woman consents to is an act of intercourse with her *husband,* not just with any man.

Some of our states have special statutes making intercourse obtained by fraud or by impersonating the woman's husband rape, but even in these states there are cases going both ways, and it seems Texas is especially rigorous in demanding that the stratagem of the man be active and not a mere mistake on the part of the woman (such as erroneously thinking that the panting but otherwise silent interloper in her bed is her husband).

Thus in an old Texas case two married women were asleep in different beds in the same room, waiting for their absent husbands to come home. Ed Huffman came home first and got in the wrong bed, that is, in the bed of his friend Andrew's

sleeping wife, Fannie. As Fannie testified later at Ed's trial
for rape:

"As soon as he got in bed he whispered in my ear and said,
'Turn over, Fannie.' . . . I thought it was my husband,
Andrew. . . . [Then] I said, 'Andrew, did you get that
meat, kerosene and stuff?' and he answered, 'No, I thought
I'd wait until tomorrow.' . . . Before I [could turn] over
[he] . . . raised one of my legs and . . . [entered] . . .
me from behind. . . . [Then] I heard . . . [defend-
ant's] wife Florence say, 'Ed, what makes you treat me this
way?' and I thought Ed was in bed with her, and that she was
talking to him about being so late. When she said this . . .
[defendant stopped] and lay over on his back still for a moment. I still thought it was my husband there with me, and
thought he [stopped because] . . . he did not want Ed and
Florence to discover [us having] . . . intercourse. . . .

"Then when Florence . . . [spoke the same way again]
and defendant began to get up . . . I discovered it was Ed
Huffman . . . and not my husband . . . and I sprang at
him and beat him and abused him every way I could. . . .
Ed said he had made a mistake and got in the wrong bed.
His wife said, 'No you didn't — you have lived with me too
long not to know the difference between me and Fannie.' "

In the trial court Huffman was swiftly convicted of rape by
impersonation, under the statute, but on appeal his conviction
was reversed on the ground that, while the wife was obviously
mistaken, the defendant had not himself used sufficient stratagem to induce her to believe him her husband and thus make
it rape.

That there are limits of latitude even in Texas is shown by
a rather touching earlier case in which a surprised Mrs.
Womack awoke one night not only to find a man in bed with
her but upon her, attempting to have intercourse. "Mr.
Womack?" she respectfully inquired. "Yes," he whispered in
reply, settling down to his work. Presumably less absorbed

than he in the enterprise she next inquired, "How is Granpa Young?" "About like he was," came the whispered reply. "What time is it?" she inquired. "I don't know," he panted. "When did you leave Granpa?" she persisted. "I don't know," he repeated. "I don't believe this is Mr. Womack," she then said, later testifying, "whereupon I pushed him away and said I would see who it was. He got out of bed [and] . . . went for the back door. . . . I followed him and . . . by the skylight [saw] . . . it was . . . Henry Ledbetter.

"I at once hallooed and said to him 'Henry Ledbetter, you vile wretch, you shall pay for this with your life!' " Since the defendant was convicted of rape, and stayed convicted, and rape is a capital offense in Texas, which has capital punishment, she just may have been right in her macabre prediction, although the report does not say. But if there is any essential difference between this case and the Huffman case it is so subtle it has eluded me.

True, in this case, to her direct question whether he was Mr. Womack the man answered yes, but in the Huffman case, especially during the brief gabble about the groceries, the man did virtually the same thing, that is, played along with her erroneous assumption, now known to him, that he was her husband. In this area of the law it seems a man must carefully choose his words in order to remain out of prison.

This moderately well-traveled participant in and observer of the human comedy, though scarcely advocating either rape or indiscriminate bundling, does find it rather incredible that even a faintly virtuous woman could for long mistake a strange man in bed with her for her ever-lovin' husband, and especially so in that closest, most intimate, elemental and secret physical embrace that can occur between a man and a woman. Is it possible that some of the Texas judges have anticipated my skepticism and, having repented of the past, tacitly decided to boycott what they may consider a well-intentioned but wrong-headed act of the legislature? Could be, could be. Or perhaps the masculine ego simply cannot endure the thought that any woman anywhere could possibly ever mistake a strange man for that unique irresistible musk-ox of a male she married. Come to think of it, it *isn't* very flattering.

One of the strangest — and saddest — cases in this whole strange realm of rape by husband-impersonation (strange enough to make the plot of a bad best-selling novel) was a Scottish "Enoch Arden" case (with a twist) decided back in 1926. In 1918 a Scottish war bride called Margaret Anderson lost her young husband, a member of the Royal Scots Fusiliers, in France, and in due course he was officially reported killed in action.

Eventually she was remarried — to a William Baxter of Glasgow. Then in August 1925 a strange man showed up at their home and told her he was her "late" husband, James Anderson; that he had been captured by the Germans and had after many vicissitudes only recently returned to Scotland. He so far convinced her with his story that then and there he bedded her in her own home. But he lied; in fact the man was an imaginative impostor called Montgomery. When his masquerade was penetrated he was indicted for rape under a statute similar to those existing in several of the United States providing that a man who induces a married woman to engage him sexually by impersonating her husband shall be deemed guilty of rape.

The defendant Montgomery objected strenuously to the indictment, arguing that since the woman was lawfully married to Baxter and he had not impersonated her husband Baxter but a *dead* man who was her *former* husband, the statute clearly did not apply and the indictment was bad. The court wrestled and cogitated — and, I suspect, also consulted the Zodiac, if not the entrails of a freshly killed chicken — and finally held that if the woman believed he was her first husband, and that accordingly her second marriage to Baxter was invalid because innocently bigamous, and, while thus mistaken, she consented to lie with him, the statute was violated and the man would be guilty of rape.

This is as refined and tormented a construction of an "impersonation" statute as I have yet discovered, on a par perhaps with some of the finest-spun metaphysical musings that have emanated from Scotland in the past. To my mind the decision injects a dangerous subjective test of guilt that plainly was not written into the statute or ever contemplated by it. Only Hollywood could have dreamed up such an eventuality. One suspects that the outraged judges were consulting their prayer books rather more assiduously than their lawbooks to reach such a devious result — and one says this regardless of the admittedly scoundrelly behavior of the bad (or too good?) actor Montgomery.

In this general realm of rape by fraud and impersonation, one detects in the cases a somewhat greater tendency to convict when the "consent" is granted by a woman who thinks she is submitting to something other than intercourse (such as phony medical treatment or, as we have seen, advanced voice culture) than when she knowingly "consents" to the mutually anticipated act of intercourse for fraudulent reasons, such as phony marriages or husband impersonation.

L'ENVOI: There must be a moral lurking in all this for the wandering hotbloods of America, and in the unlikely event that any of them can hold still long enough to read this or any book, perhaps I can best conclude the seminar by giving them my best guess as to what that moral might be.

Moral: If you *must* crawl into the sack with a strange sleeping woman, don't do it in Missouri and don't have made any previous side deals with her husband, as it will avail you not and may land both of you in prison. Above all, before commencing hostilities be sure first to wake her up and when she murmurs sleepily, "Is that you, dear?" don't say, "Yes," but merely grunt. Following these simple ground rules may in the long run save you a lot of *time*.

12

Remember the Alimony

ADULTERY is the classic ground for divorce nearly everywhere, at least one virtuous jurisdiction once making it the only ground, while in others it merely heads a long indulgent list of grounds that seems occasionally to include eating crackers in bed. But adultery, where it is alleged, must still be proved in open court, it still takes evidence of the fact, and all of us have heard or read about those prearranged little tableaux that are staged to furnish that evidence, where the erring spouse and his or her compliant bedfellow obligingly pose for waiting sleuths or conveniently stationed flash-bulb photographers. "LOVE NEST RAIDED IN BRONX!" Remember those titillating headlines?

But there is a certain aura of tawdriness in such melodramatic goings-on, not to mention the expense of enacting these sordid little dramas and the frequent extent and nastiness of the ensuing publicity. Hence of late years the more sedate of aggrieved spouses who suspect their mates of marital infidelity prefer gathering their evidence by less flamboyant means. One of the commonest ways is for the wife to hire a private detective to tail her suspected husband to help prove her case. Since one out of five marriages are said to end in divorce, the private eye has come into his own in recent years, and not only fictionally; a lucrative industry has grown up around his activities. But who pays the busy private eye for his pains when his work is done?

Usually the erring husband does, and he does so most often on one of two broad legal grounds: first, on the old English common-law theory that a husband is always liable for the "necessaries" furnished to his wife, and that under proper circumstances hiring the services of a detective to track him down may become a pressing necessity. The second ground springs from the equally ancient legal doctrine that a divorce court, being a court of equity, has an inherent right to award the wife "suit money" to protect her interests when she quarrels in court with her husband — although some courts are reluctant to extend this latter concept to include paying detective fees.

Since divorce has become one of our most popular indoor games, the lawbooks accordingly bulge with cases wherein the wife or her detective have pressed the erring husband, ironically enough, to pay the very man who got the goods on him. Most of these claims for fees have been successfully prosecuted, not only for the reasons just noted, but for the additional reason — according to some critical legal observers — that our judges in divorce cases are too often prone to adopt the punitive role of an avenging advocate; that their frequently unrealistic decisions are too much shot with misguided sentimentality and a kind of adolescent gallantry; that their awed veneration for Womanhood seems to increase in inverse proportion as they piously conceive that a particular woman, however grasping and preposterous her demands, has been degraded and put upon. "If you don't believe us," these critics in effect wind up, "contemplate, if you can, that scandalous modern phenomenon known as Awarding Alimony." (One suspects that some of these caustic critics have themselves been ground exceeding small in the matrimonial mill.)

Be this as it may, not all of these claims for detective fees have been successful; judges on occasion have given their fellow males a break. Sometimes the shadow has been left in the shade, as it were. Consider the case of *Lanyon's Detective Agency v. Cochrane*.

John and Emma Cochrane were not getting along and had not been getting along for years. They had been married in Chicago about twenty years before their first open rupture. They had one daughter. This break, during which they lived apart for two years, occurred prior to their moving to New York. Once in New York, evidently with some idea of reconciliation in mind, they took an expensive apartment out on Long Island. The following spring the wife and daughter left for California — the wife claiming later that her husband had ordered them there. After an absence of several months they came East again and were met in New York in July by the husband, who installed them in a big expensive New York hotel. They lived there for about a month, but John Cochrane did not join them and only occasionally dined with them. Things went rapidly from bad to worse.

In September John Cochrane suddenly appeared at the hotel and bluntly told his wife that he was going to leave her, that he loved another woman, and that he was never coming back to her. To make it unmistakably clear that he meant what he said, he repeated it and then abruptly left. The wife and daughter thereupon moved out to the Long Island apartment, which they still maintained, and shortly thereafter, in December, the wife brought an action against her husband for a judicial separation (virtually tantamount to a divorce except that the legal bonds of matrimony are not severed) on the grounds of abandonment and cruelty, based upon his past behavior, including what he had recently told her about loving another woman and so forth.

John Cochrane did not contest the action for separation and meanwhile provided his wife and daughter with the Long Island apartment and plenty of money as well as open charge accounts at two of New York's better department stores. Before filing her action, but after the husband had confessed his

love for another woman, Emma Cochrane hired a detective to
tail her husband to learn about his infidelities. This the detective did from October nineteenth to February twentieth, filing
an elaborate report with his client, who amended her bill of
complaint to set out an impressive list of the husband's infidelities, complete with dates and places. John Cochrane answered nothing and denied nothing, nor did he come home.

The case came on for trial and, being uncontested, the wife
routinely won her decree of separation on the ground of
abandonment, the judge also awarding her $8,000 a year ali-
mony — this back in the Twenties, mind, when a buck was
still a buck! — whereupon everyone presumably lived unhap-
pily ever after. All but the detective, that is; he still hadn't
been paid for his work.

So in a separate and later action, the detective sued John
Cochrane for his money, alleging the old familiar ground that
his services to the wife had been necessary to enable her to
protect her rights and win the separation she sought. The detective's case was tried in city court in New York, where the
detective appeared and testified how the wife had asked him
"to find out whether there was any other woman in the case,
if so, who she was, all about her, [and] how long this inti-
macy had been going on." He added that he had richly suc-
ceeded and when the smoke of litigation had settled the detective had won his suit.

John Cochrane was evidently a man of strong likes and
dislikes, and moreover he apparently didn't like the man who
had been so hot on his trail; at any rate he promptly appealed
to the appellate division of the supreme court, where, after a
long wrangle, once again he lost. Now thoroughly aroused, he
again appealed, this time to the court of appeals, the end of
the legal line for him. The case was argued hotly and heavily
briefed, and in due course Justice Crane delivered the opinion
of the court.

His Honor reviewed the facts in detail. He conceded that
the prevailing rule was that, in a proper case, a detective's

services could indeed be a "necessary" payable by the husband. He pointed out that the wife's suit, however, had not been an action for absolute divorce on the ground of adultery (the only ground then existing therefor in New York) but rather for a judicial separation on the grounds of abandonment and cruelty.

"What she found out [about his adulterous behavior] she discovered through the detective," the judge went on. "[His] cruelty . . . consisted not in these promiscuous acts of intercourse . . . but in his treatment of his wife and the things he said to her. She did not need the detective to prove [this] . . . . She . . . could have testified to it in court without the aid . . . of the detective. His work was not necessary to enable the wife to maintain her action of separation. . . . She did not need the details of his wanderings, or the details and places of his nightly escapades, to justify her action. . . . Judgments reversed."

Despite the fact that the great Benjamin Cardozo, then still sitting on that court, filed a dissent without opinion, one inclines not to disagree too strongly with the final result on its facts. The wife *could* have sought an absolute divorce on the grounds of adultery, in which event she would doubtless have needed the detective's services to prove her case — and the detective in turn would doubtless have won his separate suit for fees. But she chose *not* to file for absolute divorce, or to amend her pending bill for one, and one can only speculate whether her reasons were religious or whether, as has commonly happened, she was acting the familiar role of the woman spurned who refuses to give her erring mate his legal freedom to wed her rival. She may have not shared the cynic's belief that matrimony is often the worst enemy of romance, and that she might well have punished him more had she freed him to wed again.

It is true, as Justice Crane broadly hinted in a portion of his opinion I have not quoted, that the "goods" she got on her husband through her detective might have encouraged him not to contest her case (which would thus air all the dirt) and moreover not to fight the handsome allowance of alimony. In such situations the detective's dossier can become a kind of bargaining pawn in a sort of "pay up — or else" game of genteel blackmail. To that extent, then, what her detective did may obliquely have helped her, and one speculates that this might have been the basis for Cardozo's undefined dissent.

But the fact remains that she still did not *need* the detective's help to win the only thing she was looking for, namely, a judicial separation because of abandonment and cruelty. All the rest was fetching coals to Newcastle; her husband had already richly furnished her with all the fuel she needed. And having rather ostentatiously elected to pursue the former husband as his debtor, the detective could not very well subsequently turn around and go after the former wife. In other words, to mangle a metaphor, the private eye was left holding the bag. But all was not melancholy and rue; the poor man did not go entirely unrewarded; presumably he still had all those exciting addresses and phone numbers he had so doggedly dug up.

> *When spouses have rifts,*
> *What happens to gifts?*

This bit of doggerel poses a good question because when marriages go on the rocks the problem of whacking up the wedding presents between the warring principals has given quite a few judges quite a lot of headaches.

A fairly recent New York case neatly indicates the problems that can beset a judge in this troubled area. The opinion also exhibits one of the rarest things in the law: a genuine sense of judicial humor. In it, the feuding wife sued the feuding husband in conversion to recover the value of furniture, furnishings and personal effects which she claimed were being illegally kept by him but which belonged exclusively to her, having been purchased either with her own money or from wedding gifts in cash given her almost entirely by relatives and friends on her "side" of the family. The husband countered that most of the disputed property came from cash wedding gifts given by his "side."

The harried judge listened patiently to the evidence and to all of the claims and counterclaims, and then remarked plaintively that the authorities seemed to be as mixed as they were elusive. "Indeed I find that only Emily Post presumes to speak with confidence in this regard," he said. "[She says] 'Wedding presents are all sent to the bride and are, according to law, her personal property. . . . The bridegroom seldom receives presents. Even those who care about him in particular and have never met his bride, send their presents to her.' "

Commenting on "Justice" Post's dictum, the judge noted wistfully that not all wedding guests have been trained in the niceties of "polite" society and that regrettably many of them had not read Miss Post's book, and that furthermore there was a modern tendency to give money instead of things and that in the average wedding it was not unusual for each "side" to deliver the money into the hands of its own.

"While no one will challenge Miss Post's eminence as an arbiter of good taste," he wryly continued, "I doubt that her pronouncement on the law in this regard may be accorded the dignity of stare decisis. It would have been nice had she cited a competent judicial decision of such sweeping magnitude. Had she done so there would be no need for this opinion."

His Honor now boldly forsakes Emily Post and lays down a working rule of his own: "The time has come," he declares, taking the plunge, "to say clearly that all wedding gifts whether from the bride's 'side' or from the groom's — excepting [only] such items which are particularly adaptable to the personal use of either spouse, and those gifts which are . . . [clearly] . . . 'earmarked' . . . for . . . one or the other — commonly intended for general use in the household, are the joint property of both parties to the marriage. This [rule applies to like things] . . . purchased with cash wedding gifts not otherwise 'earmarked.' " Having "overruled" Emily and delivered himself, the judge concluded that while the wife's remedy might lie elsewhere, it was not to be found in his court on a theory that she owned the whole boodle.

In other words the judge laid down a judicial presumption that, in the absence of the special circumstances he had noted, *all* wedding gifts from whichever "side" are presumed to be given jointly to both spouses. They own them fifty-fifty. Yet in a still more recent English case the court of appeals rejected any such presumption, questioned the soundness of the New York case, and plumped for the rule that wedding gifts and money go to that spouse of the "side" from whence they came. (What the rule should be in the not-uncommon situation where the bride and groom happen to share adoring friends in common is not grappled with.) Each rule has the redeeming advantage of simplicity, but the trouble is that no one rule seems to fit every situation and each can in particular circumstances work a hardship on one spouse or the other. And so the battle rages. . . .

Nor need the prickly question of ownership of wedding presents always arise between feuding spouses. Others get into the act. Thus in federal court in a recent case arising from Arkansas there had been a divorce and then the former wife died. Her administrator then sued the former husband for certain property, including wedding gifts which it was claimed belonged exclusively to the wife and accordingly to her estate. The defendant husband fought back and showed that the gifts, mostly silverware, had been purchased and given by his own employees, who did not know the wife before he married her. He won his case. This seems to follow the English rule. Again in an earlier English case the hassle was between the divorced husband's trustee in bankruptcy seeking assets from the former wife consisting partly of wedding gifts given to her. She prevailed, yet if the court had followed the "New York" rule, one supposes she would have had to cough up roughly half of them or half their value.

Litigation costs money, especially appellate litigation, yet alienated spouses continue to fight rancorously down to the wire over items that are often obviously worth but a fraction of the cost of battling over them. Pride seems to be an element; perhaps that and just plain cussedness. Thus in a recent "wedding gift" case in Massachusetts the articles fought over embraced such matchless treasures as an old vacuum cleaner and two iron plant holders that the husband had given the wife before their marriage during a "bridal shower." The court held that the wife owns exclusively all gifts given her at such prenuptial showers, and accordingly she emerged triumphant with the coveted vacuum cleaner and the two plant holders. What price glory? Perhaps there is a moral in all this for prospective brides: Contrive if you can to get most of your wedding loot at "bridal showers" — at least in Massachusetts.

Though the courts frequently disagree on precisely how to divide the disputed swag, they generally agree that personal stuff that the other could not very well wear or use goes to the spouse who can, regardless of which "side" gave it. Thus, in a recent Pennsylvania case the husband managed to keep his cuff links while the bride clung to her jeweled bracelet. In an old Michigan case the husband, who had lost his divorce case, nevertheless emerged from the fray bearing aloft the following priceless pearls: an old brass cuspidor, a used poker set, a rocking chair, an icebox, a fishing rod and reel, an old shaving cup and three packs of cards.

Greater triumph hath no man won, and it is heartening to know that in this uncertain world it is still given to learned and begowned men of the law to devote themselves to grappling with such cosmic profundities. The deathless opening couplet having now been answered, it should probably be amended and enlarged. Here goes.

When spouses have rifts,
They fight over gifts.
Full of rancor and rue,
They hire lawyers and sue.

13

The Injustice Mills

SAM Thompson, an old resident of Louisville, Kentucky, was on his way home one Saturday evening in January 1959. It was about six-twenty and he decided to stop in at the Liberty End Cafe, one of his favorite spots, and have himself a beer and a plate of macaroni while waiting for his bus, which was not due until seven-thirty. It being the dinner hour on a Saturday night, the place was fairly jumping, with customers coming and going, dishes rattling and glasses clinking, the busy waitress running to and fro. Through it all the jukebox blared its thumping din.

Finishing his snack, Sam noted that he still had about a half hour to wait so he listened to the raucous jukebox, keeping time to it with his foot. At this juncture two Louisville policemen happened in, one of whom went over and spoke to the manager, sitting on a nearby stool, and then went up to Sam and asked him what he was doing in the place.

"Waitin' on a bus," Sam replied.

The officer thereupon arrested Sam for loitering, contrary to the city ordinance, and took him outside. There Sam put up an argument over his arrest, whereupon the officers promptly arrested him a second time for disorderly conduct, also contrary to a city ordinance. This was not Sam's first brush with the Louisville police. Over the years, in fact, there had been over fifty, most of which Sam had stoically accepted as the hand of fate. But this time Sam decided to fight. He was arraigned before the judge in police court and pleaded not guilty, got himself a lawyer and fought the two charges down to the wire.

At his brief trial, held before the police magistrate without a jury, the two arresting officers testified that they had stopped in at the cafe around seven o'clock on a "routine check" and found Sam "out there on the floor dancing by himself," one of the officers adding that, in response to his questions, the manager told him that Sam had been there "a little over a half hour and that he had not bought anything" and that he (the officer) had then accosted Sam and "asked him his reason for being in there and he said he was waiting on a bus." Both officers also told of Sam's arguing with them outside over his arrest inside for loitering and how they again arrested him, this time for disorderly conduct.

The Louisville "loitering" ordinance under which Sam was prosecuted provided partly as follows: "It shall be unlawful for any person . . . without visible means of support, or who cannot give a satisfactory account of himself . . . to sleep, lie, loaf, or trespass in or about any . . . building . . . in the City . . . without . . . the consent of the owner or controller. . . . "

At this juncture Sam's lawyer moved for a dismissal of both charges against him (loitering and disorderly conduct) on the grounds that there was no evidence to support any finding of guilt; that these latest arrests and prosecutions were police reprisals against his client because Sam had once or twice dared put up a fight against previous baseless arrests; and that to convict him now would have to be done without evidence and solely upon his past record of arrests, all of which would be to deprive him of property and liberty without due process of law under the fourteenth amendment of the Constitution. Unimpressed, His Honor denied the motion and Sam was put to his defense. It should be added that throughout the trial everybody — lawyers, witnesses, Sam himself — stood before the bench.

Sam then told his brief story: how he had stopped off at the cafe for a snack and a beer and had remained there waiting for his bus; that he had money with him and, while far from being rich, did odd jobs for various people and had worked off and on for one family for thirty years and had always somehow managed to get by.

Sam then called the cafe manager, who testified that Sam was a frequent patron in his place and had never been unwelcome; that he saw nothing objectionable in Sam's "standing there in the middle of the floor and patting his foot" to the jukebox; and that he had not told the officer that Sam had not bought anything, as the officer had claimed, but rather that he, the manager, had not sold it to him, but that someone else might well have served him. (This was one of the few disputed factual issues in the case.)

There was no police rebuttal made to this testimony and Sam's lawyer again moved the police judge for dismissal on the same grounds as he had earlier, which was again denied. The prosecution then put in the long record of Sam's previous arrests and, the case finally in, Sam was convicted promptly on both charges and fined ten dollars on each.

An aroused Sam Thompson and his lawyer were now more determined to fight than ever, but they found themselves in a dreadful bind: Kentucky statutes provided that police-court fines of less than twenty dollars on a single charge were unappealable or unreviewable in any other Kentucky court. If they paid the fines to keep Sam out of jail the case would become "moot"; if, instead, Sam went to jail to preserve his rights, his case would likewise again become moot because his fines would have long been "served out" — at the rate of two dollars a day — before he could present elsewhere his due process contentions — namely, that he had wrongfully been convicted without any evidence. What Sam needed, and badly, to preserve his rights was a stay of execution of the judgments so that he could have a decent chance to get his case to Washington, where he and his attorney determined to go if they could. So he asked the magistrate who had just convicted him for such a stay. His Honor granted him twenty four hours, the maximum allowed by law.

This was obviously not enough time even to prepare the necessary papers, so Sam and his harried lawyer swung into swift action. They went into circuit court and asked for a longer stay, which was granted. The prosecution, its own dander up, appealed this grant of a longer stay to the Kentucky court of appeals, which after a big argument granted a longer stay on its own. Shufflin' Sam was on his way to Washington.

There Sam's case duly landed, accompanied by four lawyers, two from Louisville and two more from Washington. Not to be outdone, the prosecution also showed up with a like array of legal talent. Voluminous briefs were filed, erudite arguments made, searching questions asked. The case was finally submitted. Time passed, as it has a way of doing, and one day Mr. Justice Black delivered the unanimous opinion of the United States Supreme Court:

"In addition to the fact that the petitioner [Sam] proved he had 'visible means of support,' " he said, after reviewing the background facts and quoting the pertinent portion of the Louisville "loitering" ordinance, "the prosecutor at trial said 'This is a loitering charge here. There is no charge of no visible means of support.' Accordingly he could only have been convicted of [loitering] for being unable (1) to give a satisfactory account of himself (2) while loitering in the cafe (3) without the consent of the manager. Under the words of the ordinance itself if the evidence fails to prove all three elements . . . the conviction is not supported by evidence [and violates] . . . due process of law."

Turning the judicial searchlight on this, His Honor continued: "The undisputed evidence of the manager . . . was that petitioner [Sam] was welcome there . . . and that he did not at any time . . . object to anything petitioner was doing and that he never saw anything . . . that would cause any objection. . . . There simply is no semblance of evidence . . . [of guilt]."

He pointed out that whether Sam was "dancing with himself" as the police claimed or merely doing a sort of stationary soft-shoe shuffle, as Sam claimed, was largely academic because nobody on either side claimed that solo dancing ever constituted "loitering" under the Louisville ordinance.

There still remained Sam's disorderly conduct conviction to be dealt with, and His Honor got on with that: "The only evidence of 'disorderly conduct' was the single statement of the policeman that after the petitioner was arrested and taken out of the cafe he was very argumentative." Pointing out that there was no testimony that Sam engaged in any loud talk, offensive language, resisting of the officers, or had done anything "to adversely affect the good order and tranquillity of the City of Louisville," he continued: "[all that] . . . the record contains about what petitioner was 'argumentative' about is his statement that he asked the officers 'what they arrested me for.' " He disposed of this by noting that Kentucky case law itself holds that if a man fails to object to a wrongful arrest he has waived it. His Honor was now ready to make his decision, and make it he did:

"Thus we find no evidence whatever in the record to support these convictions. . . . [It is] . . . a violation of due process to convict and punish a man without evidence of his guilt. . . . Reversed and remanded."

ADDENDUM: Since writing the foregoing I have learned elsewhere that, as I suspected all along, Sam Thompson is a Negro; that, lovely irony, he was languishing in jail on still another charge the very day he won his Supreme Court victory; that the old case was never again pressed against him; that the Kentucky legislature has since provided for appeal in *all* police-court cases; and finally that Shufflin' Sam Thompson is still alive and as full of beans as ever.

It would be wrong to conclude that the ordinances under which Sam Thompson was prosecuted were peculiar to Louisville; most municipalities have them or something like them, and indeed need them, else life in our large cities would be even less endurable than it is. What was wrong with Sam's case was not so much with the laws but with the attempt to apply them to a man and a situation they clearly did not fit and, worse yet, in persisting in the error and convicting an innocent man without evidence.

But again this danger is not unique to Louisville. Every day, in every big city, long lines of the poor and bewildered and rejected file before harried and overworked police magistrates. Is it any wonder that, confronted by such unending waves of human misery, poverty and degradation, our city police judges tend to indulge in presumptions of guilt rather than of innocence, that a kind of defensive cynicism replaces any real judicial concern, that the rights of the individual become lost finally in this endless shuffle of petty vice and human misery, that the ritual of arraignment rapidly degenerates into assembly-line justice, that the rare contested case readily becomes a grotesque parody of a trial? And if some of these glutted police courts can truly be called "injustice mills," is it not as much due to the sheer weight of woe they must daily grapple with as to those occasional instances of official malevolence or stupidity?

Viewed thus, perhaps one who has himself beheld some of these injustice mills grinding relentlessly away need not be accused of defending what happened in Sam's case if he expresses some wonder, not so much over the sketchy trial he did get, but rather that in the circumstances his trial was as good as it was. I speak of the trial itself, not the result.

For the sad truth is that most of the swarms of moochers and drunks and scufflers and loiterers and pilferers and assorted waifs who daily parade before our police courts *are* guilty, if that is precisely the word — "guilty of being born" might be more accurate — and the decision in Thompson cannot alter that bitter reality of our exploding and anonymous urban society. Moreover, one suspects that most city cops have quite enough to do keeping the show on the road and trying to cope with the gales of real crime and turmoil all around them without trumping up phony charges.

All that Sam Thompson's case can do is prod those who must deal with this daily avalanche of misery to be more discriminating, more alert to the occasional Sam Thompsons who may innocently find themselves caught up in the landslide. Did I say that this is "all" the decision can do? I didn't quite mean that. This is quite a day's work in any judicial league. And it is the one big memorable lesson of Thompson. "Keep grinding away as you must at your crime mills," the case seems to say, "but look out for your Sam Thompsons. We are watching and we care."

The decision in Thompson has been criticized for a variety of reasons: that it constitutes a further unwarranted erosion and invasion of state's rights; that our highest court has no constitutional license to concern itself with evidence or its weight or sufficiency; that it constitutes an invalid and unworkable extension of the concept of due process; that it is a dangerous excursion into the realm of "natural law"; that it will undermine confidence in the Court; that this new concern with "little" people will turn the Court into a kind of glorified police court — one might spin out the indictment for paragraphs and moreover buttress it with resonant authority. For if there is one sure thing left under the sun it is that if one searches long enough, one can find legal authority for almost any proposition one may care or dare to urge; if you can conjure it up, some judge somewhere has probably held it. Indeed, that is one of the lessons of this book.

One also wonders what the inarticulate Sam Thompsons of our land might reply to all this criticism. Might not some of them be tempted to scratch their heads and say: "Look, I don't know nothing about all them laws and fancy cases. But I do know I wasn't bothering anybody or doing anything bad — just standing there keeping time to the juke box and waiting on my bus. Yet they up and pinched me and took me away and found me guilty. Just answer me this, man: if in my troubles I couldn't have looked to our boss court up there in Washington, tell me, man, where in hell else could I have turned?" Facing up to that question might just possibly stump a hell of a lot of erudite critics who wouldn't be caught dead riding in a bus or shuffling to the beat of a gaudy jukebox.

These critics of whom I have just spoken are for the most part earnest and learned souls honestly troubled by the wrong direction they think the Court is taking, by its undeniable recent preoccupation with such troublesome things as individual and civil rights and criminal procedures and similar prickly concerns which for so many comfortable years, rightly or wrongly, were swept under the rug or left to the discretion of the individual states. Rarely if ever do these critics impugn the integrity or motives — or patriotism — of the Court or its members, and almost invariably they base even their most searching criticisms upon reason and at least debatable legal authority. This of course is in the oldest tradition of American dissent and nobody questions that.

But there are, on the other hand, various noisy swarms of what one might charitably call visceral critics: the chronic gripers and grousers, the mindless and the embittered, resentful people who once got a traffic ticket and have ever since had it in for the law, indignant and rich little old ladies in soiled tennis shoes, belligerent states' rightists, the congenital scenters of dark conspiracies everywhere, those who yearn for a return to the womb or to universal sheepherding, or both, and all the extreme groups, whether left or right. . . .

Though as diverse as our population, these curious people seem united in one thing: in thinking that the Court is soft on Communism, coddles our criminals, and is generally plunging

us to hell in a homemade handbasket, and that some or all of
its members should be impeached. In a word, that the Court
is swiftly becoming totalitarian. Rarely do these people give
or heed reason; never do they cite a case.

It seems never to occur to these poor troubled souls that in
an age when state-worshiping totalitarian regimes have
stolen and perverted the traditional language of democracy
almost beyond recognition, and are relentlessly bent upon re-
ducing the lone individual to zero, the highest court in our
land (taking Sam Thompson as an example) has heard and
heeded the solitary plea of an obscure Negro handyman and
ringingly reaffirmed the ancient proposition — won over the
centuries by cascades of blood, sweat and tears — that no
man among us (these critics included) may be convicted and
punished without evidence. The exact opposite, in other
words, of what we *know* to be daily totalitarian practice.

Those who defend the new drift of the Court also have
their little batteries of cases ready to cite, to be sure. Some of
them seem additionally to sense, however dimly, that what
the "new" Court is about couldn't be stopped whether they or
it wanted to. They too can uncork their own share of rhetorical sonorities. "Can you not perceive," they incline to intone,
"that not only the law but our country is in the midst of an
exciting new ferment; that indeed our whole Western society
is in the grip of one of those grand climacterics of man; that
we can no longer continue to live in a world of half rich and
half poor, of half privilege and half privation, of nay-sayers
and yea-sayers; that we and the world are caught up in one of
those resistless social and political upheavals that engulf
mankind every few centuries? Can you not see," they thun-
der, "that one of the linchpins of this new awareness and concern is that we, here, now — in this century, in this decade —
must either learn finally to respect the individual, the lone
man and his rights, or perish?"

Sam Thompson's case cuts to the very guts of this dream
called democracy. Besides saying once again that no man

may be convicted and punished without evidence, it implicitly reaffirms some other basic hard-won concepts: that the mere arrest and charging of a man with a crime is not enough, that the assembled power and authority of a prosecuting arm of the state is not enough, that producing a record of a man's past misdeeds is not enough, that his eccentric behavior or obscure station is not enough, that the happenstance of his color is not enough, that the presumption of innocence still means what it says, and that — above all — there is still a tribunal in this country where every man may turn for a fair shake when the going gets too rough. To say that this is "wrong" legally may in the abstract be an arguable proposition among men of the law; to say that it is wrong politically, morally and socially is for oneself to utter the dreariest totalitarian nonsense.

Despite the rhetorical glow and rhapsodic overtones of some of the foregoing I do not wish to imply that the Court can do no wrong. It can and occasionally does stumble magnificently. Perfection there is sometimes quite as elusive and fitful as elsewhere with the works of man. Packing a lawyer off to Washington and clapping him into a black nightshirt and thenceforth reverently calling him Mister Justice makes him no less fallible and uncertain that he was when he was back home drafting ten-dollar wills. Solutions do not burst upon him like a sonnet nor does his proximity to vast libraries alone make him a good judge. There must be a happy concurrence of certain indefinable qualities of heart and mind. And remember, his errors reverberate more. Thus I regard the majority decision of the Court in the recent Ginzburg "obscene" book case as little short of calamitous and aberrant in its stoic wrong-headedness. Of the decision it may be said what Mayor La Guardia once wryly said about himself: "When I make a mistake, it's a beaut!" By the same token, the Court is often "right" — in fact, in my book I regard its batting average as remarkably high — and I for one think it was dead right in Thompson.

Lord Acton once despairingly wrote: "Power tends to corrupt; absolute power corrupts absolutely." I think he might have added a more hopeful corollary: "All tyrants fall and absolute tyrants fall absolutely." Perhaps Sam Thompson's case "shewes," as Bacon once pungently said of another tyrant: "He doth like the ape that, the higher he clymbes, the more he shewes his ars." And eventually falls on it.

14

The Lady Has the Last Word

IT was past midnight on a raw windy night late in March when I finished writing this book. Dying embers still glowed in the Franklin stove and the wind grieved in the chimney. I turned off my solitary desk light and sat staring into the fire, flexing my cramped fingers, experiencing that mingled feeling of euphoria and depletion — and, yes, of sadness — that sweeps over a writer when he has finally finished his book. An exacting friend, a trying but exhilarating guest, has departed, and, along with a sense of relief, one feels curiously bereft and forlorn.

I surveyed the mound of neatly stacked and paper-clipped manuscript on my desk. It was sobering to reflect that during my little raid on the "vast neglected boneyard" of the law I had mentioned in my Preface, I had barely scratched the surface. It occurred to me that in truth I could as well have written an even bigger book on *other* phases of the law, or could indeed have written much the same book using still *other* cases. Could not a thrilling history of mankind and his aspirations and manifold follies be re-created from the thousands upon thousands of heaped and mildewing law books lying in this neglected boneyard? Well, maybe I had made a modest start.

Ah yes, the Jealous Mistress. . . . In the dim light I reached over and patted the manuscript, "her" manuscript. For a moment I was tempted to take up my pen and add a little more and thus perhaps delay the bittersweet parting. Maybe I could write something nostalgic and a little sentimental — something, say, in the florid vein with which the mellow-voiced Travelogue man Fitzpatrick used to end his movies of far places: "And so we take leave of The Jealous Mistress, and as her regal figure slowly recedes in the fading afterglow . . ." That sort of thing. Something real lump-in-the-throatish and corny.

Instead, like any sensible soul, I arose, yawned and stretched, and tiptoed my way through the silent house out to the pantry. There I built myself a massive highball, pausing, judiciously calibrating, and then adding a dividend for the road. Then, balancing my treasure, I shuffled back to my den for a solitary celebration of the occasion. *My book was over and done!* Lone celebrants are apt to do droll things, and I sat in the semi-darkness alternately sipping my drink and dipping my glass to the finished manuscript. "Here's to you, Jealous Mistress," I toasted.

It had been many hours since I had eaten, and presently I became wrapped in a warm beneficent glow, sipping, toasting, staring into the dying fire, listening to the cardiac tickings and murmurings of the faltering old Thomas family clock, drowsily listening to the searching wind still grieving in the chimney. Suddenly there was a whoosh of wind, a gusty down draft in the chimney, the glowing embers burst briefly into flame, and by its fleeting light I saw the shrouded dim figure of a woman sitting quietly in my old leather chair in the far corner. She was watching me coolly, silently, intently. Then for the first time I became aware of an odd perfume in the room, the moldy damp mushroomy odor of musty old law books. Startled, I peered closer.

Though her features were somewhat obscured by undulant scarves of some filmy material, I could make out that she possessed the brave tired eyes and ravaged throat of past beauty, long flown. Out of compassion I looked away, back at the fire, my mind churning, my thoughts darting and racing. Who was this strange woman calmly sitting there looking so curiously *enthroned?* I thought of the fragile ethereal Baroness Blixen — she who used to write under the name Isak Dinesen — then of my boyhood dream woman, the movie vampire Theda Bara, and even of that timeless and sinister creature, the sinuous lady in black in the old Charles Addams' cartoons. Again the fire flared briefly, I cravenly stole another look, and with a growing shock of recognition saw that *this* woman was none of these. Was she, could she possibly be . . . ?

"I beg your pardon, madam," I heard myself saying in my best company manner. "I didn't see you sitting there in that dark corner. Here, I'll turn up more light. May I go fix you a drink?"

She languidly waved a pale hand. "Please don't bother, Mr. Traver — or should I call you judge? I stopped by but for a moment and I won't be long. Moreover alcohol has always made me giddy, sometimes even a bit indiscreet, and strong light hurts my eyes. But thank you just the same. You are most gallant to an inquisitive old lady."

Her words, though commonplace enough, had an odd archaic *sound* about them, and she spoke in a sort of droning liturgical monotone.

"I — ah — I must say you have some advantage over me," I said. "You seem to know me, but I can't recall our ever meeting."

She laughed briefly, a low, throaty, ambiguous laugh. "I'm the Jealous Mistress of the Law, remember? After all, you should because in your fashion you've been courting me for over forty years. I feel you're an old beau."

I arose with an awkward clatter and made her an elaborate bow; rather too elaborate, as it turned out; I suddenly lurched forward and nearly upset my drink.

"How do you do?" I said gravely. "I am deeply honored and flattered by your visit." So moved was I by the occasion, in fact, that I observed I was swaying a little.

Again the quick low laugh. "Do sit down, you poor tired man. Large brave drinks sometimes play queer tricks on empty stomachs."

"I'm perfeckly awright," I protested, drawing myself up tall. "Li'l tired is all. Been cerebratin' at the ol' desk, you know."

"Of course you're all right, you big rugged man. And do forgive this sudden visit at such a late hour. But I was passing this way and I'd just learned you've been writing something about me, so I simply *had* to stop by to see how you were coming. Eternally curious woman, you know. Please do sit down."

I gratefully sank to my chair and, fumbling, opened my shirt at the throat. "Hot in here," I murmured, plopping my hand down on the pile of manuscript. "Just finished it tonight, only minutes ago, 'smatter of fact. Still a lot of honing and polishing to do, of course, but there always is." I plucked at the pile of manuscript. "Like to take li'l look? Sure hope you don't mind that I've named it after you."

"I know and I'm delighted and flattered," she said in that cool remote voice. "But I've just read your book, thank you. While you were making your — ah — remarkable drink."

I stared at her incredulously. "But that's impossible!" I said. Nobody could possibly scan and dismiss my months of toil *that* casually.

"Please don't be offended. I'm a fast reader and naturally I'm familiar with all your cases. Moreover, the thing mercifully isn't very long and also, while it has its sober moments, it isn't too profound. But I must say I had some — ah — visceral chuckles — oh dear me, I almost said belly laughs — particularly over your section on rape, you waggish man."

She paused and wistfully I asked the inevitable question: "How did you like it? As a whole, I mean?"

She pondered her reply. Then: "Again don't be offended and also please forgive my lapses into your colorful modern idiom — it *is* habit forming, isn't it? — but in all candor I must say that I feel you've missed the boat."

I groped for and gulped the rest of my drink and then sat there in morose silence. Then in a crushed voice: "I'm sorry, really sorry," I said. "I've worked hard on the thing and I had sort of hoped that . . ." I widened my hands and, brooding, stared at the fire. To be rejected, and so flatly, by the Jealous Mistress *herself* . . .

"Don't take it to heart. Your book is good enough as far as it goes — in fact I really rather like it. There hasn't been much *fun* in the law. . . . My main point is, it doesn't go far enough."

"What do you mean? It's a pretty rich mixture, aimed mostly at laymen, and I had to stop somewhere. After all, my readers aren't going to take the bar exams."

"I don't mean that. Rather I mean that you, like most lawyers, dwell too much in the past, are too much bemused by and obsessed with precedent, stare decisis, and what dear dead Lord So-and-So said centuries ago. I had hoped you might take the great leap into the future. Or at least a small step. But no. Yet from now on it is the *future* of the law that counts. 'The past is only prelude,' as someone has said."

I was growing a trifle irked. "I greatly regret, madam," I said, "that the few modest talents I may possess do not include that of penetrating the future. Writing about what I know is quite hard enough." I sulked and glowered in my chair, longing for another drink. Who did this cynical old girl think she was to be so airily dismissing my book for what it *wasn't?* She sounded like a book reviewer.

Again the low, faintly taunting laugh, again the oiled toneless voice. "But my dear man, the future of the law is implicit in its past — there as well as in the present state of the world. Even a child should see *that,* Judge."

Petulantly: "Please don't call me judge. I've served my

time and turned in my gown. You wouldn't taunt a parolee with his past, would you?"

Sharply: "Don't get on your high horse. The two situations are not the same and you know it. You also know that most former judges not only covet the title but clamor for it. It fairly makes 'em purr."

"I'm sorry, but I neither covet nor clamor nor crave to purr. Do tell me about the future I have missed that any child can see."

"That the law must escape its shackles, smash its mold, burst its prison" — she paused and smiled slyly — "but it's your turn to name one, you have such a ready aptitude for cliché."

I winced. "Break its bonds," I said helplessly.

"Splendid! All this and alliteration, too. Always there in the pinch, eh, Your Honor?" I hung my head. "But as I was saying," she pressed on, "the law must make a great leap into the future, dramatically enlarge its vision, in fact experience a veritable sunburst of revelation and self-knowledge."

"Why?"

"Because if it doesn't, and soon, maybe there won't be any law or litigants left to sue anybody about anything. It's as simple as that."

Faint hound-dog stirrings assailed the former district attorney. Triumphantly: "Ah, then you seek merely to enlarge your *own* domain, is that it? You crave more power?"

I had touched her and her voice rose. "More power and domain be damned!" she said scornfully. "I think only of mankind, of great blind fumbling — and possibly doomed — humanity."

I stifled a yawn, not very successfully. "You speak in lovely riddles, dear madam. Please let me have it, I can take it. Moreover I've got an early dental appointment in the morning."

"Ah, I speak of a precarious humanity and he thinks of his precarious bridgework," she murmured to herself. She sat suddenly erect in her chair. "Very well, my fatigued friend, I shall be brief."

"Thank you."

It was her turn to play prosecutor, and she pointed accusingly at me. "For many centuries The Law has been the biggest single thing that has distinguished men from beasts, right?"

"Right," I said.

"And man is the only animal who has learned to resolve his quarrels in the courtroom rather than by combat, right?"

"Right."

"And this unique feat is what men call The Law, right?"

"Right," I said, thinking of Professor Grismore relentlessly revealing The Word in his old law-school lectures in Contracts.

"And The Law is man's only alternative to tyranny and barbarism, right?"

Out of pride I simply *had* to vary the formula. "Yes, ma'am," I said.

She folded her sinewy arms in triumph. "Well, I *can* see a little into the future, and all these things are no longer enough."

I was silent for a moment. "Do tell me about it," I said. "Maybe I can add it to my book. Perhaps if I can say it badly enough people will mistake it for profound truth."

"Always shooting the little literary angles, eh, Mr. Traver?"

"I wasn't thinking of it *that* way. But I'm beginning faintly to see what you mean. Maybe if I passed the word . . . Do tell me what you see."

She brooded for a moment before she spoke. Then: "All right, I'll break my vows of silence over many centuries and tell you. It is this: Men must enlarge both their own vision and the law, and quickly, or mankind, the law, the Jealous Mistress, *everything*, may vanish from the earth."

Might all this happen before the publication of my new

book? I thought wildly. Ah, the pity of it, the futility, the waste of work . . . "My, my," I said.

"No, it won't happen before your book is published," she said sharply.

She had read my mind! "I'm sorry," I murmured contritely.

"You mean you're glad."

"I mean I'm sorry I'm glad," I said, feeling my face redden. "Please go on."

"Thank you. Up to now men could conceivably have survived without the law as we've known it. In fact some have. It wouldn't have been a pretty world, indeed far uglier than it is, but men could have endured and persevered and somehow — what is the current idiom? — kept the show on the road."

"I'm listening."

"Not so any longer. Today, now, in this waning century, possibly in this decade, mankind has run out of alternatives. No longer is there any choice about what men must do."

I wagged my head. "Parlous state," I murmured. "Pretty bleak outlook."

She pressed on. "When men kill each other singly they call it murder, do they not?"

"Yes, ma'am."

"But when they kill each other in droves, they call it war, their opponents dogs, their comrades patriots, their slain heroes, do they not?"

Ah, just another bleeding heart, I thought, another sensitive aching soul. "War is hell," I said sententiously.

"So it follows as the night the day that from now on war, killing, invasion — all international violence — must be regarded for what it is: the worst possible crime against humanity and, moreover, must be made amenable to Law."

"But how in the world are you — "

"Stop! Remember, I can read your mind. You're thinking the old girl's a bleeding heart, gone balmy, off her rocker, lost her cool."

"Well?"

"I now veer to the heart of it. Look, men will accept anything — do you hear? I said *anything* — as long as it becomes tribally fashionable. And whether good or bad, just as you Americans so complacently and so docilely accept along with good whiskey bad bread, with good orchestras bad television, with good roads bad education."

"Amen," I said. "Pour it on, dear lady."

She tossed her head impatiently. "I say men must now accept World Law. It's that or perish."

"But hasn't all that been tried?"

"Never. Not really. Not with men's hearts and minds and souls has it ever been tried. Ah, you are thinking it is impossible, a utopian dream. But behold the miracle of the law as we've known it. Wasn't *that* once regarded as impossible? If accepting and abiding by law could have happened to individual men in the past, why cannot entire continents and nations and races — the whole world — learn to accept the world rule of law in the future? All it takes is an unlocking of the hearts and minds of men. Every living soul is now involved and all must now help make their leaders see the light, even — and I never thought these words would come from *me* — to the point of revolt! Men can no longer remain bystanders at their fate!"

"But can this ever happen?"

"It can because it must. I repeat: men have run out of alternatives. They must banish the luxury of blind nationalism, the grotesque folly of war. It is the *only* way, man's last clear chance to survive on earth."

I sat there chilled and groped vainly for the lees of my drink. When I looked up my unbidden guest had glided soundlessly to the door. There she stood — I almost said hovered — poised, heavily veiled, regally regarding me with her tired, luminous and infinitely sad eyes.

"Is there any chance?" I murmured.

"I cannot tell for sure." She sighed and closed her eyes,

and when she went on her voice had sunk so low I had to strain forward to hear. "I see only that the road ahead forks abruptly at the horizon. One way leads to vast shining uplands where I discern men dwelling together in peace and harmony and fulfillment."

"Yes, yes?"

"While the other way — ah, the *other* — plunges abruptly into a bottomless abyss from which emanates only stifled silence and over which broods a monstrous pall of mushroom cloud."

"What does it mean?" I asked, knowing.

"It means that time is fleeing, the near road short, the fork swift, the choice both fateful and final. It means that both Man and Law face by far their greatest challenge — ah, lovely abused word for which no adequate synonym exists — during all their time on earth. I must go."

I sat staring sightlessly down at my desk. When I looked up she had disappeared. I sighed and arose and flapped my way back out to the pantry. The next morning I overslept and missed my dental appointment. Somehow it didn't seem important anymore.

References

Chapter 1

U.S. v. Rowe, 73 F.Supp. 76.

Chapter 2

State v. Coursolle, 255 Minn. 384, 97 N.W.2d 472, 75 A.L.R. 2d 755.

Chapter 3

State v. Damms, 9 Wis.2d 183, 100 N.W.2d 592, 79 A.L.R.2d 1402.

Chapter 4

People v. Dunnigan, 163 Mich. 349, 128 N.W. 180. Escobedo v. Illinois, 378 U.S. 478, 12 L.Ed.2d 977, 84 Sup.Ct. 1758; 99 A.L.R.2d 772. Miranda v. Arizona, 384 U.S. 436, 86 Sup.Ct. 1602, 16 L.Ed.2d 694.

Chapter 5

87 A.L.R.2d 649.

Chapter 6

85 A.L.R.2d 1128.

Chapter 7

Riggs v. Palmer (1889) 115 N.Y. 506, 22 N.E. 188, 5 L.R.A. 340; 36 A.L.R.2d 960.

Chapter 8

Hatfield v. Gazette Printing Company, 103 Kan. 513, 175 Pac. 382. Palmer v. Bennett, 83 Hun. 220, 31 N.Y.S. 567; 3 A.L.R. 1279.

Chapter 9

People v. Ring, 267 Mich. 657; 93 A.L.R. 993. Roth v. United States, 354 U.S. 476. People v. Hildabridle, 353 Mich. 562, 92 N.W.2d 6.

Chapter 10

Darneal v. State of Oklahoma, 14 Okla.Crim. 540, 174 Pac. 290, 1 A.L.R. 638.

Chapter 11

State v. Welch, 191 Mo. 179, 89 S.W. 945; 4 Ann.Cas. 681. Pollard v. State, 2 Iowa 567; 4 Ann.Cas. 685. State v. Haines, 51 La.Ann. 731, 44 L.R.A. 837; 84 A.L.R.2d 1022. State v. Carter, 66 Ariz. 12, 182 P.2d 90; 75 C.J.S. 484, note 68; 52 C.J. 1037, note 79; 84 A.L.R. 2d 1017; 91 A.L.R.2d 591.

Chapter 12

Lanyon's Detective Agency v. Cochrane, 240 N.Y. 274, 148 N.E. 520, 41 A.L.R. 1432; 75 A.L.R.2d 1365.

Chapter 13

Thompson v. Louisville, 362 U.S. 199, 4 L.Ed.2d 654, 80 Sup.Ct. 624, 80 A.L.R.2d 1355; 74 Harv. L. Rev. 108; 59 Mich. L. Rev. 306; 39 Conn. Bar Jour. 405.